# Writers' Workshop

## Related Titles of Interest

**Ready for Reading: A Handbook for Parents of Preschoolers**
Ashley Bishop, Ruth Helen Yopp, Hallie Kay Yopp
ISBN: 0-205-28791-3

**Early Childhood Language Arts, Second Edition**
Mary Renck Jalongo
ISBN: 0-205-27377-7

**Literacy's Beginnings: Supporting Young Readers and Writers, Third Edition**
Lea M. McGee and Donald J. Richgels
ISBN: 0-205-29931-8

**You Never Asked Me to Read: Useful Assessment of Reading and Writing Problems**
Jay Simmons
ISBN: 0-205-28854-5

# Writers' Workshop

## Reflections of Elementary and Middle School Teachers

*Edited by*

# BOBBIE A. SOLLEY

*Middle Tennessee State University*

**Allyn and Bacon**

Boston • London • Toronto • Sydney • Tokyo • Singapore

*Series editor:* Arnis E. Burvikovs
*Series editorial assistant:* Bridget Keane
*Marketing manager:* Brad Parkins
*Manufacturing buyer:* Suzanne Lareau

Copyright © 2000 by Allyn & Bacon
A Pearson Education Company
Needham Heights, MA 02494

Internet: www.abacon.com

**Library of Congress Cataloging-in-Publication Data**

Writers' workshop : reflections of elementary and middle school
   teachers / edited by Bobbie A. Solley
      p.    cm.
   Includes bibliographical references (p. ) and index.
   ISBN 0-205-29015-9
    1. Creative writing (Elementary education)   2. English language—
Composition and exercises—Study and teaching (Elementary)
3. Creative writing (Middle school)   4. English language—
Composition and exercises—Study and teaching (Middle school)
I. Solley, Bobbie A.
LB1576.W734    1999
372.62'3—dc21                              99-39588
                                               CIP

Printed in the United States of America
10 9 8 7 6 5 4 3 2 1    03 02 01 00 99

# Contents

# Foreword

Most of us who have conducted successful writers' workshops know the procedures cannot be reduced to a set of attitudes and simple steps. We also know that learning to conduct a writers' workshop is not just a matter of following the suggestions of Donald Graves, Lucy Calkins, Nancie Atwell, or any one of many excellent process-writing authors. We agree with Graves when he so eloquently writes that we must develop the craft of becoming writers ourselves and of increasing our ability to teach writing.

This book has been designed in an accessible and enjoyable manner that will be helpful to readers new to the writers' workshop and to readers who know a great deal already but who want to know more. For some time I have been feeling the need for more books on writing written by classroom teachers. Every day I teach and meet teachers who treat the writers' workshop like I do food. I have read extensively about caloric values, fat grams, and carbohydrates and yet I have made few changes in my eating plan. I know many classroom teachers, some of whom I have taught in language arts courses, who possess much knowledge about a process-writing classroom but who have made few changes in their language arts program.

Therefore, I have spent a great deal of time reflecting on the issue of how to nudge teachers into implementing process writers' workshops. The problem of conducting a writers' workshop vexes many classroom teachers, and I have come to the conclusion that it is because much of the success depends on both external sources and upon themselves. Not only do you, the teacher, need to know the rudiments of process writing, but much support is needed from administrators. Becoming a good writing teacher requires experimentation and risk taking as one moves away from the security of a teacher-directed, product-driven writing curriculum complete with story starters.

This book, written by classroom teachers who are doing writers' workshop every day, is well grounded in theory. All of the authors were guided by the great process-writing educators of the last decade. The honesty is refreshing and the revelation by each of the authors that all ideas do not work all of the time resulted from reflection about classroom practice. The editor, Bobbie A. Solley, was an excellent classroom teacher for many years and this inside knowledge has shaped the book content in a practical style.

It is well known that writers' workshops develop writers but many students are not in process-writing classrooms. My hope is that this book will give many teachers confidence and courage to take the necessary plunge into the deep water of a writers' workshop. Also, after reading this book, classroom teachers will be able to pursue their own classroom research as they consider new ways of teaching and experiment with new ideas. The suggestions of the book's authors will help them avoid blind alleys and holes in the pavement.

Although primarily intended for classroom teachers and teacher education students, this book deserves a wider audience: elementary school administrators, language arts supervisors, staff developers, teacher educators—all those interested in the implementation of writers' workshops.

To write a foreword for such a book is a pleasure indeed. I encourage the authors to continue their deep reflection and writing and to share their experiences with the profession.

Maryann Murphy Manning
University of Alabama at Birmingham

# Preface

The technique of writers' workshop has been a topic in education for many years. Although the success of writers' workshop has been documented, teachers continue to struggle with its implementation. Because writers' workshop requires a restructuring of the classroom environment and an adjustment to one's beliefs concerning teaching and learning, the teacher's role in the classroom must change. Teachers are no longer sole controlling agents who make all the decisions. They now work in concert with their children to make decisions that will benefit all. They must view children as capable decision makers. Teachers become the facilitators of knowledge and guides for young authors, rather than simply dispensers of knowledge. For some, this is difficult and overwhelming. Given the fact that state governments have taken over our schools and forced accountability based on standardized test scores, teachers are doubly fearful of losing control. The uncertainty and fear together may become so intense that rejection of the entire approach may occur.

This book is written with these challenges in mind. Teachers who are currently implementing writers' workshop are the authors. They will share their stories, their struggles, their difficulties, and their successes. They will share their beliefs about how children learn to write and how writers' workshop promotes their beliefs. The book is designed to demonstrate that teachers at all grade levels face similar struggles and frustrations, but they can be overcome. Strategies and techniques used in writers' workshop will be discussed. Excitement and enthusiasm is evident throughout each chapter. Teachers and children are excited about writing. Although problems occur, the thrill of watching children develop their writing ability overshadows the difficulties.

In general, teachers are an isolated group of professionals spending the majority of their time in classrooms with children. There is very little time to seek guidance and support from fellow educators. In implementing and utilizing writers' workshop, the need for collegial support is tremendous. Not only are teachers restructuring their classroom environments, they are also restructuring their ways of thinking. The chapters in this book are designed to support and encourage teachers. They serve as reference and support for teachers who are currently involved in writers' workshop. In addition, they serve as an instrument of encouragement to those teachers who are seeking a more effective way to teach writing. For those teachers who are just beginning, the book lends itself to the promotion of writers' workshop. Hopefully, the book will be of great strength to fellow classroom educators.

*The most distinctive feature of the book is that it is written by teachers who are presently utilizing writers' workshop. Each contributing author focuses on an aspect of writers' workshop she has had particular success with and/or aspects that have been difficult to handle.* Throughout each teacher's journey you will see not only the growth she experiences teaching writing, but you will also witness each teacher's personal discovery of herself as a writer. It is in the belief of one's self as a writer that a person can truly become an effective teacher. While some of the solutions to struggles may be obvious to some teachers, they are not to others. Again, this demonstrates the journey we all travel as we struggle to become effective teachers of the writer.

The success of writers' workshop is evident as teachers discuss children's growth in writing over time. First grade children's progress with invented spelling as well as the relationship between invented spelling and writing are discussed. Rehearsal and topic selection are discussed as upper grade children struggle to find their writer's voice. Attitudes change and develop as children of all ages are given the opportunity to write, share, and think.

In addition to the successes that teachers encounter, the book also deals with the difficulties of writers' workshop. The difficulty children face when rehearsing is discussed. Several teachers discuss the conflict between doing what they know to be best for children and being forced to abide by state and local curriculum guidelines that do not coincide with "best" practices. Still other teachers examine the difficulties with classroom setup, managing conferences, conducting meaningful mini-lessons, and developing effective assessment. The writers' workshop is not without its difficulties. But, as you will see from these teacher-authors, the problems can be solved in meaningful ways that benefit children.

*A second distinctive feature of this book is the fact that it is written by teachers who teach in grades 1 through 8.* The chapters in this book will demonstrate how children at all levels can and do benefit from writers' workshop. While each author writes about her own particular grade level, the techniques used and the problems encountered may cover a range of grade levels. The techniques and solutions that one author uses may be viable for a number of grade levels. While not all the authors will agree on appropriate solutions to problems, all will agree that writers' workshop works when utilized in ways that meet the teachers' beliefs as well as the children's interests and needs.

The book contains eight chapters. The first chapter is an introduction, in which writing is discussed and a brief history of the research is included. In addition, an overview of writers' workshop is given. Each of the following chapters is written by an elementary or middle school teacher. The teachers have experience ranging in duration from three to sixteen years. Their experience with writers' workshop ranges from one to six years. The topics within each chapter vary according to the particular struggles and achievements of each teacher.

An appendix is included. It contains various forms and checklists the teacher-authors feel might be helpful to fellow educators. These include examples of teacher-developed mini-lessons, record-keeping forms, assessment rubrics, conference sheets, and editing checklists.

# Acknowledgments

I wish to thank several people without whom this book would not have been possible. First and foremost, I wish to thank the contributing authors. Each one has taught me much about the teaching of writing. While I sit in my university office and read and study research and theory, these seven teachers have taught me what it means to be in the "real world" of teaching on a daily basis. It is to them that credit should be given for the hard work and dedication they give to education.

I would also like to thank my editor, Virginia Lanigan, and her assistant editor, Bridget Keane. They both have been kind and gentle with me as they walked me through my first book. Thank you for the many questions and suggestions that you gave me in order to make this book useful for teachers.

My appreciation goes to the following reviewers for their input on the manuscript: Suzanne T. Mears, Hanover County Public Schools, Ashland, Virginia; Sabrina Kotts, Morrison Elementary School, Athens, Ohio; and Mary Jane Boudreau, Newton, Massachusetts.

A special thank you goes to Dr. Willis Means and Dr. Kathleen Glascott-Burriss. Countless hours were spent reading my drafts and editing my revisions. You gave me help and support that went above and beyond the call of duty. Without your help, I could have never gotten through the last year. Thank you for being my friends.

Finally, I would like to thank two very important people in my life. From the earliest time I can remember they have loved me, supported me, and encouraged me. They made me believe in myself and my ability to do anything I set my mind to, that there was nothing I couldn't do. It is to them that my success as an educator can be attributed. Thank you, Mother and Dad.

# CHAPTER 1

# Writing: Past, Present, and Future

## Bobbie A. Solley

I have been an educator since 1979, when I graduated from a small liberal arts college in the South. Beginning with my first year and continuing throughout the next nineteen years of my career as a classroom teacher, then as a graduate student assistant, and finally as a university professor, the teaching of language arts has been my focus. Writing instruction, in particular, has been my passion.

During this time, the instruction of writing has received a fair amount of discussion both inside and outside the ranks of education. Debates began in the early 1980s among educators, state and federal legislators, school board members, and parents over issues ranging from what writing involves to how writing should be taught to the teaching of spelling and grammar as precursors to writing. Questions were asked that demanded definitive answers. What is writing? How do children learn to write? When should the teaching of writing begin? Can first grade children really write? Should children be able to spell correctly before they write? What is the importance of spelling in children's writing? Should we teach grammar? If so, should it be taught separately or in concert with writing?

Although research in the area of writing has been conducted and many of these questions have been answered over the past twenty-five years, controversy continues. The major area of contention lies within the actual instruction of writing. Should writing be taught as a process with the tools of writing taught within context? Or should the tools of writing (grammar, parts of speech, mechanics, and spelling) be taught first and writing instruction later? The continued controversy has forced the polarization of issues among teachers. Sides have been taken and "wars" have been waged over writing: the tools it takes to become an effective writer, appropriate strategies by which to teach children to write, and the place that grammar and mechanics hold in this instruction. While these instructional wars rage on, however, children may be suffering.

For twenty-five years, research has examined writing and its implications for instruction. The results have provided us with knowledge concerning the process of writing, and subsequently with information about how a process-based approach to teaching writing may be a more effective instructional model than is a traditional skills-oriented "English" classroom (Calkins, 1983; Elbow, 1973; Emig, 1971; Graves, 1983; Harste, Woodward, & Burke, 1984). Despite the research, resistance to change from traditional approaches of teaching English to more effective ways of teaching children to become writers remains. Traditional approaches involve the teaching of isolated formal grammar, spelling, and mechanics instruction. The belief is that, if mastered, children will become effective writers. Therefore, in many areas of the country, teaching writing through a process-based approach continues to be viewed as a radical innovation that not every teacher embraces.

So the wars rage on between proponents of writing process and proponents of traditional skills teaching, although research supports the former. Where have we been in the area of writing research? How far have we come? What do we know now that we did not know twenty-five years ago? And what kind of impact on classroom instruction should there have been?

## The Writing Process Movement

The writing process movement began in the early 1970s with the work of Janet Emig (1971). Prior to this time, writing had been taught, measured, and assessed on the basis of an end product. Generally, students were given topics to write about and a time limit in which to write. The final product was then judged to be acceptable or unacceptable based on the instructor's criteria. Criteria included correct grammar usage, mechanics, spelling, and handwriting. Questions concerning what writers actually do during the composing process or how the process could be facilitated through instruction in the classroom were rare (Perl, 1983).

Emig (1971), in contrast to studying writing samples, began to interview and observe high school students as they engaged in the process of writing. She talked with them, asked questions, and listened as they talked to themselves. She discovered that high school students were not passive and silent during the writing process. They were actively engaged in various thinking processes as they wrote. Writers actually thought and participated in their writing *as they were writing*. They asked themselves questions, made comments to themselves, and made judgments about words and ideas to include. Emig found that writers actively engage in *thinking* as they write. Therefore, it is not only the end product that shows us something about writers and may direct our instructional decisions, but rather, it is what goes on inside writers' minds as they write that becomes an important indicator for instruction.

Emig's (1971) seminal work with high school students led other researchers to examine more closely the process that is at work when writers write. Peter Elbow (1973) introduced the idea of meaning found within a student's writing and described the importance in communication. It is this meaning, he argued, that may and should be responded to by another author. He fostered the notion of the teacherless writers' group, whereby writers sit together and discuss their writing. In this way writers are able to focus on the meaning and the message the writer has attempted to communicate. These teacherless writers' groups were the precursors to student-directed conferences practiced in many of today's classrooms.

As Emig (1971), Elbow (1973), and others focused their attention on secondary school students, Harste, Woodard, and Burke (1984) began exploring the thinking processes of preschoolers. Similar findings were discovered. Preschoolers and young writers, in their attempts to understand print, were also found to ask themselves questions and "talk" to themselves, much like secondary school writers. The move toward a process-oriented belief of writing led educators to believe that writing should be encouraged and promoted on a continual basis. Applebee (1984) examined the extent to which writing was being encouraged in classrooms and discovered that very little writing was actually being done. Although research supported writing as process, the relationship of research to classroom practice was lacking.

Research into children's writing process continued, and as it did two distinct views began to emerge. In the early 1980s a cognitivist perspective of the writing process became prominent (Bereiter, 1980; Flower & Hayes, 1981; Scardamalia, 1982). From a cognitivist perspective, "... writing is a problem-solving act, for which writers develop metacognitive strategies" (Shanklin, 1991, p. 48). Flower and Hayes (1981) introduced the idea of think-aloud protocols to understand the thought processes of children and adults as they write. The discovery of these metacognitive strategies led to a tentative model of the writing process. The process included planning, translating, and reviewing, all of which had direct implications for classroom practice. They could be taught to children through direct instruction and modeling.

A second view began to take shape in the mid- to late 1980s as more research into the thinking process of young writers emerged. Graves (1983) extended the Flower and Hayes (1981) concept of think-aloud protocols and began observing and talking with young children as they wrote. Calkins (1983) soon followed in Graves's footsteps by listening to kindergarten children. Because of the knowledge gained from these researchers, a second view of the writing process became prevalent and has probably had the most profound influence on instruction in elementary classrooms today. Social contextualism (Shanklin, 1991) involves the belief that the writing process is a naturally recurring cycle of thought. In order to support this recursive nature of the process, writers need free choice with topics that evolve from authentic experiences within a social community of learners (Shanklin, 1991). The writing process involves stages of thought that require ownership and control on the part of the writer. From a social contextualist perspective, therefore, the writing process was modified and expanded from its initial model to include rehearsal, drafting, revising, and editing (Calkins, 1983; Graves, 1983; Murray, 1978).

Researchers beginning with Emig (1971) and continuing through to the present have had a profound influence on writing instruction today. It was through the work of Graves (1983) and Calkins (1987), in particular, that the need for change in classroom environments was made evident. In order to gain the much-needed component of ownership and control, the classroom environment should be one that invites children to write. In an environment where children are in control of their own thought processes, instruction can be facilitated and growth becomes possible. Within the process, meaning takes the forefront and the product becomes a result of the message to be communicated. The classroom environment that promotes ownership, freedom, and instruction when appropriate is the classroom environment that encourages effective writers.

## Writers' Workshop

An environment that promotes effective writing instruction may exist through the writers' workshop, a term coined by Calkins (1986) and Graves (1983) and later expanded by Atwell (1987). Writers' workshop refers to a process-oriented environment. Writing is primary and the tools of writing are taught in the context of "real" writing. Different from a traditional "skills" approach of teaching the tools of writing, the writers' workshop is a place where children are given extended periods of time in which to write. They are given freedom to take responsibility for their own writing. Children become authors. The traditional classroom is a place where children are given time to memorize rules and identify parts of speech. They remain responsible to the teacher for their learning. They seldom, if ever, write. These children do not become writers. It is a matter of how we come to view writing.

If we can view writing as a process of using language to discover meaning for ourselves and others (Murray, 1978) and involving operations of the mind and spirit that consist of putting one's thoughts together into words (Moffett, 1983) then we can view writing as a craft. Just as art is a craft, writing involves a process of shaping material toward an end. The artist spends much time in crafting her art. She takes time to mold and shape her craft toward an end, that end being a finished painting. She allows herself to take risks, to make mistakes, to refine, and to begin again. The artist must have time to spend with her craft. The time that she devotes varies with the subject for which she is working. Finally, the artist must have a guide to assist in the refining of her craft when necessary.

The author, as the artist, must allow time to craft his message. Thoughts and feelings must be molded and shaped into a coherent piece of writing. The skills of writing develop through practice and effort as the message is crafted. Just like the artist, the writer must listen to his own information, make changes, reorganize, and shape his writing toward some end. The end is the message to be communicated to an audience. Writing requires a willingness on the part of the author to take risks, make mistakes, mold and shape a piece of writing. As with the artist, the writer must have a guide to facilitate the process toward communication.

The term *workshop* connotes a place where someone comes to work on her craft. The artist has a studio where all supplies and materials are readily available; a place where she can focus and spend time crafting the art. In the case of writing, children also need a place to work on their craft—a place where they can focus and spend time crafting their writing. This place is the classroom. The classroom environment must be one that encourages and promotes the craft of writing. Particular components will nurture the writing process.

A primary necessity within a writers' workshop is the establishment of a community of writers. A community is a place where children feel safe and secure in their surroundings; a place where trust and respect is established early in the school year; a place where children feel comfortable to take risks, make mistakes, and seek assistance. It is in this community that children have time to write, share, listen, take chances, support, and offer feedback to one another. It is only through mutual respect that this may occur. Children need to feel free to fully express their thoughts and feelings through writing. Again, this may only occur where there is a community of trust and respect. It is the teacher's responsibility to establish and maintain a sense of trust. All young writers must feel this sense of community because it is within the community that young writers will flourish.

A second ingredient to building a successful writers' workshop is a sense of ownership. Students who are encouraged to take ownership of their writing are more engaged in writing than children who are not. Ownership may be a powerful motivator if allowed to operate in a writers' workshop. Children need to feel that their writing belongs to them, they have control over it, and they are allowed to make decisions based on what they think is best. For too many years, teachers have felt the need to extrinsically motivate children to write. Calkins (1994) talks of her initial practices to get children to write. She tells the story of finding a hornet's nest over the weekend and bringing it into her classroom as a means of helping children get started with their writing. She was excited about it and believed her students would also be excited. To her amazement, many were not. The stories she received were bland and uneventful. The problem was that the event or motivator belonged to Calkins, not to the children. Children have much to tell us and much to share in their writing if we will only allow them to take the ownership and control they need.

A writers' workshop requires that children be given choices. Choices may include topic selection, genre, length of the piece, when it is time to conference, how they will go through the process, and the time they expend on each phase. They need to make decisions for themselves concerning the audience they will appeal to and when and where they will share their piece. Responsibility generates from this decision-making process. Children need to take responsibility for their own ideas and their own writing. Once children know and understand that the responsibility of writing rests with them, they begin to take pride in their work. They begin to show respect for themselves and the pieces they write. With responsibility comes intrinsic motivation. Children will no longer need artificial story starters. Children will become responsible for their own story starters.

Time is another important ingredient in a successful writers' workshop. There is no craft or skill we do that does not require time, effort, and practice. To become a competitive swimmer, one must spend time in building endurance, stamina, and energy levels. Extended periods of time must be given over to practice sessions where the whole of swimming is developed as well as specific parts that may need refining. The same is true for writing. To become an effective writer, time must be given to write. Frank Smith (1988) believes that children learn to write by writing. Therefore, children must have time to write in order to build a repertoire of words, thoughts, skills, and competencies. These extended periods of writing times allow children to plan and rehearse, draft and revise, conference, and proofread and edit: essential ingredients to effective writing.

Finally, a writers' workshop needs a teacher who is knowledgeable about the writing process and the need for ownership, choice, and time. He knows and understands that writers need these components in order to become effective writers. A teacher's role in the writers' workshop is very different from the role of a traditional English teacher. Whereas the traditional teacher is the authority figure dispensing knowledge to passive listeners, the writers' workshop teacher must become a coach, a guide, a direct instructor, and a facilitator. In addition, the teacher must understand the development of young writers, their need to develop at their own pace, and the instruction that must occur in order to advance individual development. Being a teacher of the writer requires a great amount of "kid-watching" (Goodman, 1978, p. 42). Teachers are constantly observing, taking notes, asking questions, listening, and watching in order to understand the nature of a child's writing so they can assist that child in becoming more proficient. The teacher in a writers' workshop is an active participant in all aspects of the workshop.

## Teachers of the Writer

I began my educational journey teaching fifth grade in a small southern town. Armed with the traditional English model, I began teaching. The process-oriented research had just begun, and little of its results had filtered into college and university classrooms. Therefore, I began teaching language arts in isolation, just as I had been taught. I came prepared with all my games and "cute" ideas to teach language arts. The idea of teaching children's writing was not considered. I believed that if I did a good job teaching the skills of grammar and mechanics to my students, in time they would be able to write with proficiency. Therefore, we spent time memorizing verb tenses, defining parts of speech, and diagramming sentences. Periodically, we would pull out the games I had made and play them in order to reinforce the various aspects of English that had been directly taught. Only rarely did my children write. My assumption was that now that I had taught them the skills, they would be able to write in future years.

I continued my professional development by gaining a master's degree, attending various workshops and inservices, and finally attending the Sunbelt Writing Institute at Auburn University. It was at Auburn that I was introduced to the works of Peter Elbow, Donald Murray, Donald Graves, and Lucy Calkins. While my knowledge was still limited, I began my journey toward more effective writing instruction by allowing my students to write. But I, like Lucy Calkins (1994), felt that children needed external motivation to write. Rather than bring in a hornet's nest, I created wonderful ideas to write about in the form of story starters. The story starters were made of beginning sentences, opening paragraphs, or scenarios that I had written on large index cards with the appropriate drawings to enhance the words. My children were given time each week to choose a story starter and write a story. Again, as Calkins discovered, the stories my children wrote were flat and unimaginative. More frightening to me, however, was that many of the students did not enjoy writing and some even refused. My journey had hit a pothole.

The research on writing continued to gain momentum, and, through my readings and work with other teachers, I began to understand the nature of the writing process and the impact the process could have on teachers and classrooms. Most significantly, I began to understand the impact the environment has on children's writing. My journey took on a life of its own as I began to appreciate that a process approach was a necessity to effective writing instruction (Elbow, 1973; Graves, 1975; Murray, 1978). I learned that the process is ongoing and must be "lived" in order to enhance writing. My children began to "live" writing and it was then that the process approach transformed my classroom into a "writers' workshop" environment wherein children were free to take responsibility for their own writing (Atwell, 1987; Calkins, 1986; Graves, 1983).

I have met many teachers throughout my career as an educator, and every one of them can relate similar journeys. I have been privileged to work with many public school teachers, both male and female, in the establishment and maintenance of writers' workshop. Seven of those teachers, all female, will contribute to this text by relating their journeys telling of their struggles, fears, and successes as they embarked on the writers' workshop. Each teacher will relate how her journey began but all will continue on paths that are dependent on each teacher's personality and each group of children. The journey is a process of ups and downs, trials and mistakes. Most of all it is a journey of discovery. With each teacher's story you will hear that journey.

Barbara Long is a first grade teacher who has been teaching for twelve years. She has been involved in the writers' workshop for the last four years and continues to grow in her understanding about the nature of young children's writing. As she attempts to address individual writers, her methods change and her repertoire of instructional techniques grows.

Rebecca Harrison is a new teacher with two years' experience. She teaches second grade and has been engaged in writers' workshop from the beginning of her career. Rebecca is one of those unique teachers who insists upon engaging her children in everything meaningful and purposeful. Writers' workshop was the first and foremost adventure that she undertook with her children. Her story will amuse and give hope for beginning teachers.

Debra Hurst-Seigfried is a veteran teacher of sixteen years, teaching grades kindergarten, first, third, fifth, and sixth. She began the writers' workshop six years ago while teaching fifth grade. Currently, she is teaching third grade and has been most successful in engaging her children in the writers' workshop at both grade levels. She states that she always wanted her children to enjoy writing. It was not until she implemented writers' workshop that this occurred.

Suze Gilbert, a sixth grade teacher, has been involved in writers' workshop for four of her five years of teaching. She tells of her goals for herself and her children and describes the many strategies attempted.

I met Tina Robertson five years ago. When introduced to the concept of writers' workshop, she was probably the most skeptical of any teacher I had met. Tina has been teaching for seven years and currently teaches sixth grade. She had to be convinced that writers' workshop actually worked to help children improve their writing. She became convinced when she began implementing it four years ago. She now sees its value and is one of writers' workshop's staunchest proponents.

Pat Reneau is another veteran teacher, of sixteen years. She currently teaches seventh grade and has been involved in the writers' workshop for two years. When I met Pat she was frustrated with her method of teaching and, consequently, with her students' nonretention of information. She states, "I wanted to teach children the skills of writing that will be useful and long-term and especially relevant to their lives. Teaching from a mandated textbook did not satisfy my needs in the teaching of writing. Writers' workshop makes children's writing personal and relevant to them."

Virginia Wadleigh has been a teacher educator for fifteen years. She teaches eighth grade and has been involved in writers' workshop for two years. Virginia's frustrations were similar to Pat's. Her children simply did not enjoy writing and, therefore, would not engage in it. She began writers' workshop in the hopes that her students would assimilate language skills better if they could see the full picture of writing. Her hope was for students to use writing to communicate. Skills would then be imbedded in the meaning.

The teachers you encounter in the following pages will tell of real classroom life. They will share with you their journeys through trials and frustrations as well as through successes and accomplishments. It is our hope that as you read the stories from these teachers you may be renewed and inspired as you endeavor to help children become more proficient writers.

# CHAPTER 2

# Writers' Workshop: Teaching Outside the Comfort Zone

## Barbara Long

*A sense of pride began to rise in Michael as he shared his first "published" book. You could see it in his eyes as they seemed to dance with anticipation. Even the way he held his book showed me that he knew he had done something special. As a teacher, nothing is more rewarding and satisfying than to see one of my students begin to achieve. No tool has helped me do this any better than the writers' workshop.*

*I remember Michael's first attempts at writing. Those early journal entries appeared to be nothing more than senseless scribbles with no recognizable letters or pictures. My earliest efforts to help him express his thoughts seemed ineffectual. It was only after nearly three months of consistent encouragement by me and the other children that the writing process began to emerge.*

*After each child in the class finishes reading that first published piece, the other children and I celebrate their accomplishment with applause. For Michael, this was especially gratifying. Michael is autistic.*

Every child deserves the opportunity to reach beyond personal limitations, to achieve his or her maximum potential. Many children are never given this chance. Too often, grades, test scores, and labels are used to determine how much children are capable of learning before they can prove their level of actual ability. Writers' workshop offers all children an opportunity to feel successful and be successful without these confinements.

*Michael listens during writers' workshop.*

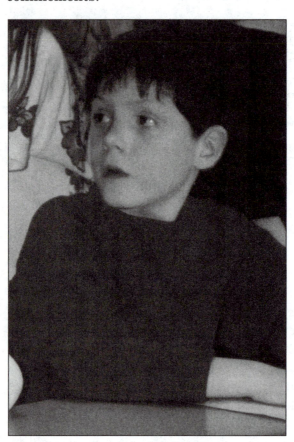

## In the Real World of the Classroom

I had been teaching first grade and prefirst for five years when I decided to return to school myself. A promised salary increase and a few good ideas were all I really hoped to receive. Little did I know that I was about to launch into an entire new approach to my career as a teacher. What began as a way for me to make more money evolved into a new professional journey.

My first introduction to writers' workshop led me to think that the professor had been out of touch with the real classroom world for far too long. She talked about ownership and empowering children to make their own decisions. We tried to explain to her that in today's classrooms children, schedules, and curriculums were not designed with those types of freedoms in mind. Children today simply could not make decisions about their own learning.

Under her leadership, however, we openly explored the concept of guiding children to develop skills as authors, spellers, and creators of books. She continually presented theories and research to support these concepts. We discussed the impact and sense of accomplishment writing might have on a child's entire education. Self-esteem and self-worth certainly affect anyone's desire to learn. What we wanted to know, however, was how to best address these issues in the classroom.

As I listened, I thought about my inner city first grade class. My initial thought was that in order to allow more freedom and ownership I would have to give up too much control in the classroom. I had always felt myself to be a reflective teacher, measuring my success by subjectively trying to evaluate the progress of my children socially, emotionally, and academically. But, in the typical inner city classroom, strict structure had always seemed imperative. I had become comfortable with that environment. If the children were given too much freedom of expression, I might lose control of the learning process.

The more I studied, however, the more I was forced to reevaluate my thinking. I discovered how much I emphasized the work outcome, the product. I began to realize that the process of learning was much more important than any end product. I also began to notice how bored the children seemed to be during certain parts of the day and had to admit that we did virtually no writing. Everything had become a routine with no room for creativity. My teaching needed to undergo some changes. I needed to stretch beyond my comfort zone.

I began to read and try new techniques. I discovered the importance of the reading-writing connection. Therefore, the first step in my journey was to build a class library. I began collecting multiple copies of trade books for the children to use in their reading groups. I featured children's authors and began showing the children how authors are real people who just took the time to express, on paper, their feelings and thoughts. I wanted them to see that they, too, could become writers so I purchased spiral notebooks for each child and began journal writing on a daily basis. I eventually revised my classroom schedule to include writers' workshop. The children were now writing and reading daily. And as they did so, it became clear to me that reading and writing should not be taught separately. I came to discover the natural connection that existed between reading and writing. The children, if allowed, would make that connection as they engaged in authentic experiences.

The results of those initial efforts were exciting. As I encouraged children to explore the realms of reading and writing, their individual reading levels skyrocketed. They began associating letters, sounds, and words to their pictures. A connection was being made. No longer were my children bored with reading and writing. They were reading books that interested them—books to which they could relate. In addition, my children were writing stories that were real and had meaning to them. For the first time in my career, I saw children take ownership of their learning. They were making connections between reading and writing at their pace, not mine.

Even though there have been many adjustments, corrections, and even some failures along the way, my philosophy as an educator has been forever changed. I began my journey from a place of security and familiarity but was forced to move outside my comfort zone in order to grow. Today I enjoy what I do more than ever before. I am not as product-oriented as I once was. I now focus on the process. I am discovering that it is the process that helps children to experience real-life learning. Besides leading my children to become authors, I am helping to produce thinkers.

No two classes of children are alike. No two children are alike. This means that every attempt to teach is unique to itself. The challenge is to guide each individual child to reach his or her potential. Learning, even for the teacher, is a lifelong process. I still don't have it all together myself but as my journey continues, I'm closer than before.

## Getting Started

In this section, I will outline the steps I use to implement the writers' workshop. Other teachers may do it differently, but I have found what works best for me in my grade level. The pictures are of first grade children actually engaged in the writing process. Try to replace the faces you see with children in your classroom. Begin to feel the excitement as they see their thoughts come to life.

### Jump Right In

I begin writers' workshop on the very first day of school. I want children to realize that writing is important and is something we do each and every day. Therefore, on that first day, I provide each child with a spiral-ringed notebook. I tell the children this notebook is their journal and each day we will be writing and drawing about things that interest us. Explanations are given concerning writers' workshop and the fun we will have as we share and learn about each other. I instruct them to write or draw anything they wish in their journal. There is no right or wrong journal entry. The purpose of journaling is to let the children know that creativity and expressiveness are valued.

As the children journal, I circulate throughout the room asking questions and making comments. "Tell me what you are writing about today." "Who are the people in your picture?" "What are the people doing?" Children respond and talk more about their pictures. By engaging children in writing and talking on that first day of school, I am able to assess their abilities to express on paper what they are feeling and experiencing in their lives. I want children to love writing. I give them freedom to write about what they are interested in and then celebrate their choices.

Many children begin their writing by drawing pictures of their family, school, pets, or anything that is currently occurring in their lives. At this early stage, few attempts are made to write actual letters or words. When a child does begin to write, I praise the effort I see being made toward the actual writing versus drawing. These first attempts at writing produce approximation. Children approximate the adult spelling of words and may reduce those words to initial and ending consonants they hear. I accept any attempt a child makes. I want all children to feel success and accomplishment. I want them to understand that they can take risks and learn from their mistakes.

### In the Beginning

Once children have been journaling for several days, I begin to structure the writers' workshop time. Each session begins with read-aloud time. Reading aloud not only models good reading but also models good writing. Children are able to see how authors effectively draw audiences into their stories. They see and hear effective use of words and sentences and come to understand how writing is simply "talking on paper." In addition, reading opens up worlds of new and familiar experiences for children—experiences that may become topics for future writing. Children have many things to say and experiences to tell. Sometimes it takes a nudge from a book in order to remind them of all the things they do indeed know.

**TABLE 2.1    Suggested Schedule for a Daily Writers' Workshop Session**

| | |
|---|---|
| 5 minutes | Read aloud |
| 10 minutes | Mini-lesson (as needed) |
| 5 minutes | Model your own journal entry. |
| 3 minutes | Summarize briefly what will be going on in the writing workshop today. |
| 20–30 minutes | Writing time. Teacher circulates, assesses, conferences, and encourages. |
| 5 minutes | Time of celebration |

Following the read-aloud time, on my classroom marker-board or flip-chart I draw and write my own journal entry for the day. I talk through it as I work and allow children to ask questions and make comments. I make it a point to share personal things about myself. I do this for two reasons. One, the children seem to respond better to my leadership when they know more about me. I become a real person to them with a real life and real feelings with which they can identify. Two, by seeing and hearing what I share, they begin to understand better what their journals should look like. This is new to most of my first graders, and it helps to see examples of writing and drawing.

As they talk, question, and listen, children begin to hear and recognize thought processes that occur when we write. They then feel more confident to engage in their own journal writing. By talking aloud as I write, I am also able to introduce simple decoding and letter writing. I sometimes ask children to help me sound out words. For first graders who are just learning about letter–sound correspondence, I find this especially helpful. Through these demonstrations, children observe me as I struggle to come up with ideas and struggle to sound out words. Hopefully, they begin to realize that it is okay for them to struggle as they attempt to write. Making mistakes is a part of learning. It is only in a risk-free environment that children feel free to try new things, make mistakes, and learn from them.

In addition to the modeling, I also use this time to teach. These informal mini-lessons provide children with the necessary skills to become good writers. Mini-lessons may concern themselves with the mechanics of writing such as punctuation and spelling. They may also focus on the crafts that make writing better. These may include adding detail, using descriptive words, sequencing, and the like. Again, this time is spent talking and questioning. Children are as much a part of the teaching as is the teacher.

I am able to teach meaningful lessons as the children ask questions and make comments while I write my journal entry. They come to understand that talk is a part of writing. Writers' workshop encourages planned free times for the children to think and talk among themselves. During this time children are free to move around and talk to their neighbors concerning their writing. Many teachers have difficulty with such nonstructured moments in their schedules. I, too, had difficulty with this aspect of the workshop and was forced to step out of my comfort zone. I had been accustomed to a quiet, structured, teacher-led environment. I realized the importance of talk, however, and discovered that writers' workshop does not work well in a classroom where children are not given the freedom to discuss things among themselves. Therefore, I had to work with the children in order to find a comfortable noise level in which we could write. As a class, we decided which behaviors were acceptable and which were not. We established boundaries for free talking times whereby children were allowed to talk only about their writing. Through these class discussions, decisions were made that helped us establish a sense of ownership for all members of the class.

One of the significant benefits of these talking times is that children become the teachers. I find I am needed less as children take ownership of themselves and one another. For example, a child might ask me, "What letters say (/th/)?" But before I can respond, another child might answer, "t-h." My input as the teacher is not needed, and I am free to help another child. I remember being asked how to draw a picture of a house that was to appear in the distance. As I began a lengthy explanation of depth and perspective, another child simply went over to the bookshelf, got a book we had read, opened it, and said, "Look, this is how you do it." The concept was taught and understood in a matter of seconds with no help necessary from me. Children can be great teachers, too.

Life in the classroom is filled with unplanned teachable moments. Writers' workshop seems to create spontaneous opportunities to teach truths that can be applied in all curriculum areas. Be diligent to look for and use the teachable moment. It may produce some of your best teaching.

### Time to Go Deeper

The move from journaling through the entire writing process to actual publication of a work is exciting for the children. Some of the most rewarding times have been when the entire class first walks through the whole writing–publishing process together.

One of the themes I use each year is a study of the ocean and everything connected with ocean life. As we near the end of the study, the children brainstorm all the facts they have learned. I record the information they share onto sheets of newsprint. This list of thoughts and sentences is what I call the "sloppy copy," or the first draft of an actual writing project.

When all ideas have been listed, we take scissors and cut the newsprint into separate sentence strips. I allow the children to decide the sequence by putting the sentences in the order they think best tells their thoughts about the ocean. We then paste, tape, or rewrite each sentence onto a separate sheet of newsprint. This collection of sheets, or pages, is the beginning of their "final copy." I divide the children into small groups and assign each group one page of the final copy to illustrate. Each page then has a sentence and a corresponding illustration.

Once the groups have finished and all pages have been illustrated, the remaining sections of our book are completed. I brainstorm with the children some possible titles for their book. We vote for the one most popular, and the title is placed on the cover. Following the title page is an "author's page." Everyone in the class who participated signs his or her name on this page, signifying that each child is an author. Seeing their names in print helps give children ownership of the project and raises their level of self-esteem. The very last page in the book is a page for "readers' comments." As children, parents, and other teachers read the book, feedback is written on the comments page.

The book is now ready to go home with the children. Over the next few days, the newly published class book is checked out and different children take it home each night to share with parents. A note is attached that asks for comments, especially compliments, to be written on the comments page. Parents and children are encouraged to sit and read the class book together. This step in the process promotes family literacy and keeps parents abreast of what we are doing in class. Later, when the children have completed their own individual books, I encourage each child to give his book to several classmates to take home and read with parents. Again, the parents are asked to write comments that encourage the young authors.

A helpful suggestion is to laminate, if possible, all the pages of each completed book. Laminating helps preserve and protect the final product. The spine for the book can be plastic rings, yarn, or staples. The final edition needs to be durable since it will be handled repeatedly.

By working together to publish a class book, the children will have seen and participated in the full writing–publishing process. I suggest producing a class book several times during the year using various themes. Not only does participation in class books assist children in learning about the writing process, it also allows them to work in a social environment with other children. For many, this does not come naturally. Working together and working independently are both positive attributes of the writers' workshop.

### I Can Do It Myself

I follow a five-step process discussed by Lucy Calkins (1994) in her book *The Art of Teaching Writing*. This process involves six elements: rehearsal, drafting, revising, editing, publishing, and conferencing. My children are involved in some aspect of all six elements.

Rehearsal and drafting can be seen in first grade children's journal entries. Generally, they occur simultaneously as children draw and make their first attempts with writing. As I begin to see several entries in a child's journal involving the same topic, I suggest he or she consider making a book from those entries. This becomes the "sloppy copy," or first draft of a book.

Revising at this age is minimal. First graders have a difficult time stepping away from themselves in order to determine what an audience might need. Therefore, revisions take place in the sequence and details of a story. I meet with the writer and help him determine whether or not his story makes sense to an audience.

First graders are capable of engaging in simple editing. I begin by modeling how to check for writing skills, such as punctuation and capitalization. As children gain experience, they are able to edit their own work.

Publishing is the final "coming together" of all their hard work and efforts. The book becomes a finished product.

Conferencing, I have discovered, is not a separate phase but occurs throughout the writing process. I conference during rehearsal and drafting by asking questions to elicit talk. In addition, conferencing gives me a chance to model revision and editing strategies. One of my goals during conferencing is to motivate and encourage young writers. I want children to be willing to take risks, make mistakes, and learn from those mistakes. Pride and accomplishment in their work is my goal. When a child leaves a conference with me, I want her to be happy about all she has done and excited about continuing the process until it is completed.

In addition to the six phases just mentioned, I add a seventh. It is the celebration with the author for a job well done. Donald Graves (1983) calls this "Author's Chair." The author's chair allows children to share and celebrate the completion of a book.

In order to relate more fully to the writing process of first graders, I will examine several of my students' journeys. Through these children, you will see the stages of the process as they develop.

***Step 1: Drafting and Rehearsing.*** Samuel is an avid writer. He writes daily and is never at a loss for topics. As I observe Samuel writing in his journal, I notice he has several different pages about his family. I conference briefly with him and suggest he use his journal pages to write a book about family. Because he is obviously interested in that, he agrees. Samuel pulls all his "family" pages and places them in a writing folder I have provided. These pages become the beginning of Samuel's "sloppy copy." After a few days, I check his work.

*Samuel works on his "sloppy copy."*

**Step 2: Revising.**   Brittney has spent several days with her "sloppy copy." She is comfortable with it and asks for a conference with me. As Brittney sits down with me and reads her book, I ask questions, make suggestions, and check the sequence of her story. I am able to evaluate the progress of her work. The conference encourages Brittney to clarify the information as well as talk through the story line. We discuss any changes that need to be made, and Brittney returns to her desk to continue work.

*Brittney conferences with Mrs. Long.*

***Step 3: Editing.*** Editing is the time where all pictures and writing from the "sloppy copy" are transferred to the "final copy." At this time, Tabitha puts the final touches on her work, correcting all letters and words, and makes sure every picture clearly says what is it supposed to say.

To assist children in this final phase, together we create an "editing chart," a list of what needs to be included and excluded from their published works. The creation of the chart gives me a chance to teach the mechanics of good writing and the reasons behind each point we list. I keep the chart displayed in a very visible place in the classroom.

*Tabitha edits with Mrs. Long.*

***Step 4: Publishing.*** To my first graders, publishing means taking the "final copy" pages to the laminator and binding them together. Melanie completes her story, and the pages are laminated. She feels a sense of accomplishment during the publishing stage, as do others. I make sure all children understand the significance of their achievement. They have become authors. All my children feel proud of themselves for this accomplishment.

*Melanie's story is laminated and ready to publish.*

**Step 5: The Author's Chair.**    In order to celebrate a finished work, I use the author's chair. In my room I have a special chair, a place of honor, reserved just for this. As each book is completed, its author sits in the chair and reads his book to the members of the entire class, who are seated on the floor in front of the chair.

*Michael sits in the author's chair.*

The rules during author's chair are simple. While an author is reading, no one else is allowed to say or ask anything. Only after the reading is completed may children make comments, ask questions, or offer suggestions. I teach my children to raise their hands if they want to address the author. At the beginning of the year, I become one of the audience members and model how author's chair should be done. I demonstrate how to make comments and ask questions that often include statements similar to these:

> "You did a good job with your illustrations."
> "The part where the dog barked was funny."
> "Where did you get your dog?"
> "Who was that in the picture on the last page?"

As author's chair becomes more familiar to the children, I remove myself from the group as much as possible so the focus is on the author. It usually takes three or four experiences with author's chair before the class understands and begins to practice appropriate behavior. We always end this session by affirming the new author with our applause.

As a teacher, it makes me so proud to listen as children read their stories. In addition, I know that I have accomplished something wonderful as I see my children listen attentively out of respect for the author. Being seated in the author's chair is both an honor and a reward for a job well done. The author beams with pride as the children respond to his story. As a teacher, you too will feel a sense of personal accomplishment. This is one of those moments when you will be able to see tangible proof that your teaching is working and is making a difference in a child's life.

## How Do I Spell ?

As a first grade teacher one of the initial hurdles you will face in writers' workshop is the endless parade of questions about spelling. The idea behind writing at this age is to help children believe themselves to be writers. In order to encourage this belief, children need to feel free to write or draw without worrying about "correctness." When children feel pressure at the rehearsal, drafting, and revision stages of writing, they miss the opportunity to take risks in a safe environment. Fear develops. When the fear of being scolded is prevalent, children refuse to write or draw. An atmosphere of acceptance must be built. While first grade children are exploring the world of print, they will make approximations. Teachers must be willing to celebrate those approximations. By so doing, children will come to believe themselves to be writers.

Because my children are at the early stages of spelling development, I work with them to "sound out" words they want to communicate. Sandra Wilde (1990) calls this "inventive spelling." In the mind of a first grader, words look like they sound. Therefore, at the beginning of the year, I expect to see initial consonant sounds only.

*Melanie invents spelling at the beginning of the year.*

I read to my children several times each day. We write together and we write individually. My children are constantly surrounded by print. Through this daily exposure to meaningful print, children begin to recognize words. They begin to see a purpose to words. Once this occurs, the children will begin using these words correctly in their writing. More and more consonant sounds, as well as vowel sounds, are added. At this point, they are on their way to becoming independent spellers.

I want my children to take ownership and responsibility for their own spelling and writing, so I encourage them not only to "sound out" words but to use their surroundings as well. For example, not long ago one of my children walked out of the classroom and took his journal into the hallway. Just as I was about to correct him, I noticed that he was copying the word *exit* from the hallway sign. He needed to use the word *exit,* and he knew where to find it. He was using his surroundings!

In addition to using sound and environmental print, I help my children create a unique tool that has proven to be quite effective. My children create their own dictionaries. Each child receives a small memo pad. The children then write a different letter of the alphabet on each page. If a child is struggling and "needs" to know the spelling of a word, he brings his dictionary to me already turned to the correct letter page. As we talk about the word and listen to the sounds, I write the word in his dictionary. These children-created dictionaries give them a kind of "word bank" to use throughout the year. It is just another way to encourage independence.

Spelling is not just a challenge for the children. Parents ask many questions as well. I address this issue during the first parent orientation of the year. Because the children are spelling phonetically it can be a little confusing at times for parents. I caution them about becoming overly concerned as to what they see at the beginning of the year. I explain to them that spelling is developmental and progresses at a different pace for each child. I also share examples of typical first grade children's writing. I explain what to look for as their child attempts to spell. I encourage parents to examine writing for what a child can do rather than the mistakes they see. For example, Carol uses the word *people* in her story and spells it *pepl.* The word is not spelled "correctly," but she is making an approximation. Carol is listening to the sounds in the word and hears initial, ending, and middle consonants as well as long vowels. Parents need to understand that learning occurs as we build on what children know rather than on what they do not know.

Finally, I send home current articles about the writing, spelling, and reading connection. I feel it is important that parents understand the reasonings behind what I do in the class with their children. I want them to understand that spelling is very important to me; but in my class, we will approach it from a nontraditional standpoint. Children will be allowed to move through spelling stages at their own level of development. Lessons will be taught and appropriate spelling will be modeled, but only as it has relevance to what children are writing. Parents need to be made aware of that nontraditional approach. I encourage parents to call me if they have question or concerns about spelling. It is important that trust be built early between the parent, the child, and me (see Appendix 1).

## Assessment Tools

A second major challenge for me as I utilize writers' workshop is determining how to blend the rich environment of writing into the traditional system of grades and progress reports. It is important to be able to evaluate each child's progress and convey that progress to parents. Doing it in such a way that maintains the dignity of writing is difficult.

In order to be effective in my assessment of progress and growth, I use a checklist system. The system is one I created based on my professional readings and knowledge of children's writing development. I call it the "Monthly Writing Checklist" (see Appendix 2). As I move throughout the room during each session of writers' workshop, I carry a notebook of these checklists and a pack of Post-it notes. When I observe a skill or technique being utilized, I record and date that information on a Post-it note. The Post-it notes are then placed in a spiral notebook, thereby assuring me that observations have been made. Later, this gives me a reference whereby I can assess progress quickly. Once a week, I take the notes and transfer them to each child's checklist. It is virtually impossible to observe each child on a concentrated basis every day. Each week, therefore, I select four or five children to observe. This observation involves conversations and closer looks at the progress each child is making. It allows me to focus on a child for consecutive days.

Not only do these checklists serve as a record-keeping system, they also allow me to recognize strengths and areas of need. They help me better meet the specific needs of individual children. When areas of need are recognized I pull together the children who are having similar difficulties and teach a lesson. This individualization is one of the strengths of writers' workshop.

In addition to my formal record-keeping system, I file and date each child's completed journals. The journals display a sample of their writing day by day. During parent conferences I sit with both the child and her parent(s). We turn through the child's journal and make note of the progress she has made. This allows parents to see more clearly their child's writing skills emerge. It is helpful to show, firsthand, just how far the child has come in her development.

*Tabitha's writing in September.*

*Tabitha's writing in February.*

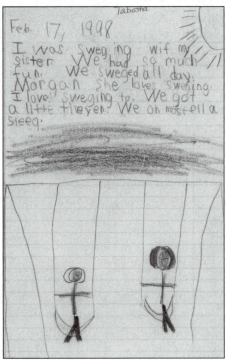

Although my foremost concern is the assessment of growth and progress, in my school district, we are required to give report cards. We are required to give each child a letter grade of E—excellent, S—satisfactory, I—improving, N—need to improve, U—unsatisfactory. The first grade report cards have a section called "writing mechanics." I use this section for my writers' workshop grade.

I evaluate each child according to his or her individual progress, using as criteria the level of participation in class, the application of writing skills, and the manipulation of the writing process. I get this information from my Post-it notes, checklists, observation notes, and completed journals. Grades can be very deceiving when evaluating any child's ability to be creative. I am very careful that I do not allow the grade to dictate or stifle any child's freedom to write. What is important to me is the observations I do as I watch writing skills emerge and develop. Reducing the richness and power of writing to a letter grade is a tragedy.

## Make It Your Own

Good educators constantly strive to enhance their classroom skills and to improve their effectiveness in guiding students to learn. Writers' workshop helps me do both. It offers an opportunity for children to explore areas in their own lives and to express effectively what they discover.

There is no right or wrong way to do what writers' workshop attempts to do. No year of writers' workshop has ever been exactly the same for me. The differing personalities within each group of children set the tone. I encourage you to begin where you are as a teacher. Design your class so that it best fits your personality and style of teaching. Do not be afraid to explore new ways of doing things. Be sensitive to where your children are. There are great rewards awaiting those who have the courage to teach outside the comfort zone.

# CHAPTER 3

# The Struggles of a New Teacher

## Rebecca Harrison

*Ashley entered second grade as a good student, but she had little knowledge of writing and its purpose. She had very little confidence in her ability to write, yet slowly she began putting her thoughts on paper. What she wrote had relevance to her; it made sense. She could write like she spoke and how she heard others speak. Ashley became empowered when she read her story and revised her mistakes. She became particularly adept at spotting spelling errors, trying to spell them in a variety of ways, and finding the correct spelling in the dictionary or other reference books. Her overall reading improved. She embraced the writing process. Ashley is now a confident writer. She continues to struggle when skills are presented in isolation, but her progress as a writer has been metamorphic. Ashley knows she is an author.*

I think how proud I am of Ashley and the entire class. Their improvement is an affirmation of the synergy of writers' workshop. However, I still look back and wonder, "Did I teach my students all they needed to know?"

## Paths I Took

I have not always been a teacher. I have, however, been a person who loves children and cares about their needs. I began my professional career in fashion merchandising and spent ten years in retail management. I changed jobs often during those years. I could not find my "place." I was unhappy and unfulfilled. After much thought and reflection, I headed back to the university, where I completed my bachelor of science degree in early childhood education and began my master's work in curriculum and instruction.

When I finally entered my own classroom for the first time I was wiser and more mature; I was ready to begin my career in education. Upon graduation, I had high aspirations of whole language, integration, and hands-on learning. The realities of the classroom, however, were much more challenging than I expected. Practicum classes and one semester of student teaching did not fully prepare me for the rigors of classroom life. The focus during college had been on developing our own philosophies of teaching. Therefore, I set out to put into practice the philosophies I espoused. Rousseau (1964) had convinced me that children are innately good. In addition, I was in accord with Montessori's (1912) beliefs that children should be allowed to experience the excitement of learning through the choices they make rather than being forced to learn what we deem essential. These two ideas became my creed. I studied child age and stage development as advocated by Piaget (1969) and Elkind (1989), and developed lessons accordingly. I wanted to live and breathe the educational credo of doing "what is best for children."

The truth, as I found it to be, was that your first year of teaching is all about survival. I found out quickly that my beliefs did not coincide with the requirements of teaching in my system. Rather than choice, I was given a list of skills mandated by the state, a stack of textbooks to use, and a roomful of children who were eager and looking to me for direction. Although grounded in my beliefs and confident in my abilities to teach, I, like many first-year teachers, taught through textbooks, not topics of interest to children. Skills were taught in isolation with little or no choice or variation.

I was in great conflict with myself that year. I wanted to teach children in ways that were appropriate, fun, and meaningful. I believed what they learned in my classroom should have immediate and direct application to their daily living. Instead, I had them reading out of textbooks and turning in worksheets. The insecurities of being a new teacher kept me from attempting many activities and experiences that I believed to be age-appropriate and effective. Seasoned teachers told me the activities I did try were "cute," and children would enjoy doing them. The reality, according to my experienced peers, however, was that those activities would not translate into higher test scores. I began to think my beliefs were only the ideals of a novice educator. I was frustrated and confused.

The summer following my "initiation" year, I began reading about the technique of writers' workshop. The issues I read surrounding writing dealt with my own—issues of choice and meaningful learning. Many of the tenets associated with writers' workshop matched my own personal beliefs. The concept that children learn to write by writing matched my belief of hands-on experiences where children actually participate in their own learning. By writing on topics of interest to them, children would have choices and find meaning in their writing. There would be real-life application to the skills and concepts of English. Because students would revise and edit their own work, they would feel successful. Self-esteem and confidence would be built. No longer would they feel anxious about what they wrote. The children would become the "teachers," refining and correcting their own work.

On the first day of my second year of teaching I began to prepare the children to write. I began with the little knowledge I had read of writers' workshop. I was excited and plunged ahead. Because of my desire to teach writing effectively and my lack of knowledge about writing, I enrolled in a university course dealing with writers' workshop. It was unlike any college class I had ever taken. Ten diverse teachers met for three hours a night, four nights a week, for three weeks. We were totally immersed in the writing experience. We began our discussions with rehearsal. We learned to live the life of a writer—to see potential writing in everything around us. The day following each class meeting, I introduced what I had learned to my students. As I learned about the writing process, so did they. I was so excited! I took each new strategy I learned and gave it a test run with my class. I wanted my students to feel the same excitement I was feeling. I was discovering, along with them, that I was a writer. I was not William Shakespeare or Tennessee Williams but I was an author with valid thoughts, feelings, and ideas worthy of being expressed in print. I wanted my students to feel the same way. I wanted them to become writers.

Even though I wanted to believe this new technique would work, I still had reservations in the back of my mind. Would it work? Would children learn the skills necessary to complete the achievement tests at the end of the year? Would they really learn to write by writing? The children, however, had no such reservations. They were thrilled at the prospect of writing and sharing. So, together we moved forward with the writers' workshop. It was trial and error taking baby steps all year. But, at the end of the year, I no longer had any reservations. Writers' workshop had been a success. My students were truly authors.

I have completed my second year of facilitating writers' workshop and continue to make changes. Certain things, however, remain constant. I conduct my writers' workshop with two main goals in mind. First, each child needs to feel he is of value. All children need to feel they are worthy and important and must be treated with respect. Second, lessons taught must be based on real-life application. Children need to learn to make decisions and to think for themselves. A child may be able to memorize and score well on a standardized test; however, if he cannot communicate his thoughts and feelings in writing, he is not prepared for life. Both goals keep me focused as I strive to promote and encourage writing.

I believe writers' workshop to be a natural extension of my feelings for children and my philosophies of child development. The classroom must be a place to experience and discuss life and all that life involves. Isn't that what school is all about, to prepare children for life? It is more logical to conduct learning in real-life experiences. Writers' workshop allows for that.

## Writing with Second Graders

Second grade is a lovely place to be. The children are full of energy. They enjoy learning. Second graders want to please the teacher, yet they are establishing their independence. For some children, establishing independence is a very natural progression from being dependent on adults for direction to depending on themselves for knowledge. For others, it is a foreign concept. To make decisions without the assistance of an adult can be frightening. Writers' workshop helps teach children independence in thought and expression. They are given the freedom to choose their own topics and progress through the writing process at their own pace. The children are encouraged when all ideas are accepted and considered valid. Once they are instructed, through minilessons, on the grammar, mechanics, and craft of writing, they have the autonomy to make changes. Writers' workshop gives children ownership of their work. Although the teacher and other students have an opportunity to offer input into the process, a child's finished work is the result of her ideas and her decisions.

One of the first decisions second graders begin to make occurs during rehearsal. Topic selection can be very disconcerting, but with time and patience can become quite easy. Rehearsal, the time when topics are selected, is quite enjoyable to second graders. The variety and simplicity of activities that encourage rehearsal allows the students to feel successful. They feel knowledgeable about their lives and the world around them. They are confident as they decide topics upon which to write. However, the transition from rehearsal into the first draft can be difficult. The hesitation to begin stems from a variety of reasons. This may be children's first experience at authentic writing. They may expect a story prompt that gives them a jump start on their writing. Because of previous work on drill and skill workbook pages, children may become conditioned to a right and a wrong answer. Therefore, there must be a right and wrong story, and he may not write the "right" one. Given the educational history of some children, it is hard for them to believe their teacher actually wants them to write about what is of interest to them. Hesitation to draft occurs temporarily. In time, trust is built between the teacher and students. First drafts become more instinctive and less forced.

The processes of revision and editing are much more difficult for second graders. They write their stories exactly as they think and as they talk. Once they have written a story, second graders believe it to be finished. Traditionally, teachers have only given students one chance to complete a writing piece before assigning a grade. Children are not accustomed to a second chance to better their work. Therefore, revision has no meaning to them. They have no prior knowledge upon which to build. Only after repetition, examples, and experience do these children make a connection to revision. By the end of the year, they look back and read their first books. They laugh at the mistakes that, in retrospect, seem obvious.

When teaching the writing process to second grade students, I find it important to keep in mind that they are between six and eight years old when they enter my room. They need lots of encouragement and guidance. Directions need to be kept simple and understandable. I take a lot of time with each aspect of the writing process. My goal is for children to feel comfortable and feel successful with each stage of the process before moving forward.

## Getting Started

From the first day my students enter the classroom, they are involved in writers' workshop. I have found it best not to label the activities in the beginning as "writing." Many of the children I teach immediately put up barriers and become fearful at the thought of writing. They have learned to read the year before, but very little writing was done. For those students who have no experience, writing a story seems an insurmountable task. Their frame of reference is the books and authors they have read.

I can almost hear the voices in their heads saying, "I can't write like Eric Carle or Marc Brown." "What am I going to do?" "I'm not good enough or smart enough." "Someone may laugh at my story!"

Because of these insecurities and the lack of writing experience, I begin with a familiar activity. Many children at this age continue to view drawing as their writing. In order to build on past experiences, therefore, I ask them to draw a picture of anything they wish, real or make-believe. The pictures range from small stick-figure drawings of their families to elaborate fantasies of monsters on the moon. I also draw a picture on chart paper. My picture is not flawless, but it does include lots of detail. I am not artistic, but I do this in order to demonstrate the process to the students. In addition to modeling, my picture shows them that their teacher is not perfect, and I do not expect perfection from them. I do, however, expect them to do their best.

After several days of drawings, I ask students to choose from their daily drawings the one they like best. I also choose one of my drawings. I then use my picture to demonstrate how to label each item in the drawing. This is the preparatory shift from drawing to print. I write mostly naming words such as *house, tree, mom,* and *me.* I find it best to keep it simple so the children won't feel overwhelmed. The students also contribute labels to my picture. When my drawing is completely labeled, the children are asked to label their pictures.

*Nicole draws herself at home on a sunny day.*

Once the pictures are labeled I begin making simple sentences with the words on my picture. This continues the transition to print. The students follow suit with sentences of their own. I then put together a simple paragraph to model form and mechanics. The children attempt the same. I accept whatever they put forth. I believe this to be critical in establishing a sense of accomplishment and confidence. We bind the products together in a booklet. It is their first finished product in writers' workshop. Second graders love to have something tangible to share with parents and friends. At this point, I explain they have completed their first book for writers' workshop. Some are excited, others bewildered. They had no idea they were "writers." It is an invaluable experience. I feel it is important to have the children complete one or two "books" in order to feel successful with writing. The purpose is to alleviate any anxiety and stress about writing before it starts. Writing is not so scary, then. The completed works are observable examples to the children that they can write. It also illustrates writing as a process. They are not expected to sit down and write a perfect story in thirty minutes. Writing occurs over time as thoughts are processed and written.

I prefer to go through several rehearsal activities at the beginning of the year then ease the children into the succeeding stages. I have discovered that rehearsal sets the stage for other writing projects throughout the year and is well worth the time spent. We learn to make lists and brainstorm from a single word or phrase. We write down memories in our journals. We take walking tours in and around our school to learn to be good observers. I may ask the children to write down the sounds they hear or the sights they see. Some tours focus on one of the five senses and some are for pure discovery. These activities prepare children for future rehearsals and writings. I am teaching them to look at the world to discover writing.

As the year progresses I move the children into more and more writing. One of the first pieces of writing we do is an autobiography. I believe children write best about what they know most about. Because autobiographies require children to write about themselves, this is where we begin. Children are able to write about their lives, their families, their hobbies, and their pets. In this way we find out about one another, which promotes the sense of community we have in the classroom. From this first autobiographical writing, children soon begin looking outside themselves to other topics of importance to them. Types of writing vary from simple fiction to fantasy to some poetry. By the end of the year, second graders have experimented with a variety of genres and feel confident in themselves as writers.

## Challenges I Face

Each new year brings obstacles to overcome. Some of my challenges may not seem unique to writers' workshop, but the workshop format presents opportunities to work toward resolutions in a productive manner. Two obstacles that I have faced and continue to struggle with are the implementation of mandated programs and the children's dependence on me. I have struggled with these challenges for the two years I have been involved in writers' workshop. I have begun to find constructive ways to resolve each problem.

## Mandated Programs

As professionals in any field, educators must consistently review research, stay current regarding methods and trends, and pioneer new techniques. There are many ideas concerning writing that are circulated through the literature. Each year I consciously have to force myself to choose only one or two new innovations; otherwise, I want to do it all and I exhaust myself by taking on too much.

Within writers' workshop there are choices to be made and new techniques to try. The first year, my focus was twofold: motivate students to love writing and develop effective mini-lessons. These areas deserved special attention because they would lay the groundwork for confidence and future learning. The following year I concentrated on establishing appropriate conferences and improving children's editing skills. Each year I take on a different aspect of writers' workshop to concentrate on and improve. Trying to perfect the entire process all at once is an impossible feat. Narrowing my focus to one or two central ideas allows me to explore a variety of approaches and discover those that work best for my children and me.

Although making choices within the actual workshop was important, a bigger issue arose as I began to implement the new program. In an already time-demanding school day, one of the first choices I had to make was finding the time to fit in writing. What programs could I juggle, consolidate, or integrate in order to incorporate writers' workshop? My biggest stumbling block to this time dilemma was with mandated programs. There is no need to debate whether certain programs should be mandated or whether teachers should be allowed to make individual instructional choices. Mandated programs are a reality. From the state, local, and school levels we are told what and how to teach. Some programs are prepackaged and have specific instructions and time constraints, while others allow for more freedom. Either way, these programs consume a large portion of my day, leaving very little time for writers' workshop. Mandated programs put my teaching skills and organizational abilities to the test. Educational time is at a premium. During the first year I began the workshop, finding the time to incorporate writing while adhering to the mandated reading basal series was difficult. As the year progressed, however, I discovered a way to incorporate my reading and language arts lessons into writing.

The basal series I use is a mandated program which requires that a sequential order of skills and stories be followed. While many of the skills and strategies presented in the basal series are appropriate, the actual lessons set forth are isolated and generally have very little to do with real life. I knew, in order for children to learn to read and write, they need to be surrounded by real print that has meaning and application in their lives. Therefore, I made a conscious effort to connect reading and writing. It was not an easy task. I struggled with making the connection for myself and then trying to make it for the children. Through the stories read I demonstrated how authors choose words, phrases, and appropriate grammar to make their stories enjoyable for an audience. I explained that when they write, they, too, must be aware of their audience. Because they are authors, they must use words and conventions that are appropriate for their audiences.

After many trials and errors, my reading and writing lessons began to flow together. I combined more and more lessons, thereby opening up larger blocks of time for children actually to read and write. By the end of the year, my second graders had begun to recognize the connection between reading and writing. They had begun to read like writers and write like readers.

Once I resolved the issue of the reading series, in the second year I incorporated writers' workshop I was required to institute a new program: a formal phonics series. Daily, children recited phonograms from flash cards and wrote them for dictation. Words were spelled phonetically and tests were given. Following strict directions in the manual, it took forty-five minutes to an hour each day to complete. I thought this was an enormous amount of time to spend in isolated phonics and spelling instruction that had little or no connection to authentic writing or reading. I felt stifled. Rote memory and repetitious dictation were not the way I felt children learned best. To me, there was no meaning or purpose in the exercises. There were no connections to daily living. For some of the students, spelling ability did increase somewhat, as well as their ability to decode new words. But at what price? The children were becoming so focused on spelling that comprehension was sacrificed. I believed phonics and spelling should be taught, but only within the context of real reading and writing and in ways that meet the needs of children. I had to devise a plan whereby the phonics program could be incorporated into writing.

Being a new teacher, I had little experience in alternative methods of teaching phonics and spelling other than in the context of real reading and writing. The only solution to my dilemma came by decreasing the time spent in the formal phonics program. I continued to teach phonics and spelling, but not in a formal, directed way. I began to teach both phonics and spelling in context. My children were taught alternative strategies for spelling other than "sounding out." I implemented a procedure I called "1-2-3 Spell." In this procedure, children focused on spelling during the editing stage of their writing. They located words they were unsure of and highlighted them. Children were then asked to take three tries at spelling the word correctly. For example, if the word was *catch,* a child might spell it *kats* or *katc* or *catsh*. The child was then instructed in the use of the dictionary and told to look up the word. In this way, I was teaching children three different strategies for spelling: listen to the sounds in words, examine the word by sight, and use the dictionary.

*Ashley and Michaela edit together by practicing "1–2–3 Spell."*

Mandated programs, for many teachers, are a fact of life. I continue to struggle with these restrictions placed on me. I continue to struggle with teaching phonics and have not fully found a viable solution. As I continue to search for ways to improve my teaching I hope to resolve the issues that surround these programs in ways that will best meet the needs of my children.

## Children's Dependence

A second problem I face each year is children's dependence on the teacher. It has been my experience, in my short tenure as a teacher, that the problem of dependency seems to increase each year. Children depend on me for their every move. They make no decisions and take very few risks. Some children are hesitant to make their own choices for fear the choices will be wrong, and they will be punished or chastised. In order to lessen this problem, I begin the year with joint decision making. In my classroom, the children and I establish rules, routines, and standards of acceptable behavior that are consistent throughout the year. This works to a certain extent. But, even though children have had input into these decisions, they continue to seek direction, permission, and assurance that the choices they make are "correct."

I want children to become good decision makers. In order to be good decision makers, however, children need opportunities to use their own judgment, try and fail, and try again without fear of reprisals. Writers' workshop empowers children to make their own decisions. They make decisions about what they will write, how long it will be, and to what type of audience it will be written. It also gives children power to make decisions in judging the worth of a piece of writing. In the beginning, children come to me with their stories and questions: "Is my story good?" Over time, as I encourage children to examine their stories to determine whether an audience will enjoy it, the children become more adept at judging their own writing. They learn to trust themselves and the decisions they make. Through these experiences, children are encouraged to take risks and make changes. It is only through this risk taking and decision making that true learning occurs.

## Lessons Learned

Writers' workshop has been a learning experience for both the children and myself. As an educator, writers' workshop has increased my awareness of the students and their abilities to write. I have become a "kid watcher" (Goodman, 1978, p.42). I observe children as they write and as they conference. My observations of students' first drafts reveal initial strengths and weaknesses. Through observations of writing, peer conferences, and listening to the questions they ask, I am able to identify more accurately areas of competency and areas of shortcomings. Subsequent one-on-one conferences during revision and editing illuminate those initial strengths and weaknesses that serve to solidify my mental notes and verify my anecdotal records. I then use the information I gain from observations in planning whole group mini-lessons, as well as individual and small group lessons.

Through writers' workshop, I have gained confidence in my abilities as an educator. I am confident in the decisions I make. I no longer fear justifying my methods of instruction or assessment practices to parents or administrators. I look forward to opportunities to demonstrate the effectiveness of writers' workshop. I am able to show parents the clarity of a child's thinking that is evident through his writing—thinking that may be masked in worksheets and test scores. By using children's writing, I can show progress in learning.

As a teacher of the writer I have learned to trust myself. I have learned to take risks. In so doing, I have made mistakes. Before writers' workshop I viewed making mistakes as a failure. I no longer maintain this view for I have discovered that true learning comes from the mistakes we make. It was my students who first helped me realize this. Often, they became upset when their writing wasn't "just right" the first time. Over and over I told them, "This is how we learn, from the mistakes we make." As the year progressed, students began to notice that I became frustrated when plans did not go "just right." At that point, students became the teacher, comforting and reassuring me, "That's how we learn, Miss Harrison." Together my students and I have grown to appreciate the mistakes we make. We have learned to focus on the meaning behind the mistakes. It has made us better learners and better writers.

Writers' workshop has become an integral part of my classroom. It reaches into every area of our curriculum. I hope to continue to make the workshop more diverse as I grow and gain experience. I want to continue focusing on strategies that foster good decision making. I believe to teach this in the context of writing will have a far-reaching impact on all areas of children's lives. At the heart of writer's workshop is my desire for my students to feel accepted and successful. They can leave second grade feeling empowered, feeling good about themselves, and knowing they are writers.

# CHAPTER 4

# The Joy of Writing

## Debbie Hurst-Seigfried

"I have a confession to make," I quietly told my class. "I have always been afraid to write. I don't feel good about my writing, and I really don't view myself as a writer."

Stunned silence filled the room until Priscilla said, "Mrs. Seigfried, you mean you have been teaching us about writing and you don't think you can write?"

She was right. It was May, and I had been teaching my students how to write all year and had never felt the joy of writing for myself. With their encouragement, however, I began sharing stories I had written. I was scared and nervous, but my students listened with love and patience, gingerly choosing their words before commenting. Their response was positive as they reassured me that I could write. A bond began to form as I opened up and showed my vulnerability. Others began to do the same. Writers' workshop took on a new life. Children had been writing all year, but now they began to truly live the life of a writer. I found I became intimate with the lives of these children through their stories. The cold hand of death had plagued some, and the tragedy of *divorce had left some feeling empty. Hurts emerged as well as joys. I had tapped into their needs, their interests, and their lives. Writing had meaning for them and for me.*

## Where I've Been

I have been a classroom teacher for more than fifteen years, with experience in grades kindergarten through sixth. Throughout my teaching career writing has always been of interest to me, but I struggled with how to teach it effectively. It has been a journey of ups and downs, trials and errors. As I moved from kindergarten to sixth grade, first to fifth, and then to third, writing has proven to be the one area that has caused me my severest frustrations but also my purest joy.

My joy came from teaching young children. For five years I taught children in kindergarten and first grade. In both grade levels, writing instruction came easily. I filled the learning centers with hands-on activities, allowing the children opportunities to label, draw, write, type, paint, or use letter stamps to create words and sentences. We wrote group experience stories for everything: first day of school, field trips, class visitors, special days, theme topics, and books we read. My students drew pictures, then wrote stories about them. They wrote in their journals daily about topics of interest to them. The room was full of excitement as children wrote, shared, and displayed their work. Everyone enjoyed writing.

My frustrations came in the upper grades. Because my expertise was in the lower grades, teaching fifth and sixth grade was uncomfortable for me. I, like many other teachers, believed fifth and sixth graders were too old to do what kindergartners and first graders had done. I knew they needed time to think, experience, and write. But, to write about a picture drawn, a book read, or a field trip experienced seemed too primary. I felt older children needed something more "mature"—something more tangible than simply writing about what they had experienced. I expected them to know how to write; all they needed was a jump start. So, I told them what to write. In centers, I provided story starter prompts or pictures to motivate creative writing stories. In addition, I set aside a time for journal writing. These were free daily writing times when students wrote about anything they wished. Eventually, these journals became nothing more than diaries of what they had experienced. They dreaded it, and I dreaded reading them. The products from both the creative story starters and their journals were dull, dry, and uninteresting. I was frustrated and confused as to why these older students did not enjoy writing or want to participate in it.

I searched for answers everywhere. I examined English textbooks and teacher's manuals. I had conversations with other upper grade teachers and searched for professional books that might help. Nothing seemed to give me the answers for which I was searching. Rather than continue seeking answers in my teacher's manuals and other outside sources, I began to look inward. What did writing mean to me? When had I learned to write? What had my teachers done to promote writing and what effect did that have on me as a writer and a teacher of writing?

I had written in elementary school, where I had been told what to write. Topics were given to me through prompts and story starters. In eighth grade, however, my teacher assigned a creative story to be written, and the topic could be whatever we chose. I wrote what I considered to be a well-written story, and when I turned in my paper, I felt a sense of accomplishment. My teacher, however, had other ideas. When she returned my story a few days later, there at the top was a large red "C." No reasons or explanations were given, just the grade. I felt defeated. My belief that I could not write became firmly implanted, and I was discouraged from ever wanting to write again.

As I continued to reflect I realized I had been greatly influenced by my teachers and how they taught writing. It began to dawn on me that I had never really been taught *how* to write. I was asked and told to write, but I was never taught how. It was at this point in time that I discovered writers' workshop. It was here that my growth began and the lives of my students changed. Writers' workshop became the instructional technique I used actually to teach my students to write. This way of teaching writing gave my students freedom to explore, take risks, make mistakes, and learn. For many, this freedom was confusing and frustrating, but once accustomed to it, they began to grow into writers with a sense of ownership. They began writing fiction, nonfiction, personal narratives, mysteries, historical fiction, plays, poems, and puppet plays. I was the facilitator who kept things going, and it was amazing what happened. They learned to write. They *wanted* to write. In fact, on days when students earned free time they asked for extra writing time as rewards. I had finally found a way to teach writing to older elementary children. It was all in the approach, the method of presenting writing to students.

I was still unsure of my own writing, so I took a course where I participated in a writers' workshop. I wrote and conferenced just like elementary school children. I rehearsed and drafted and asked for help. What slowly began to dawn on me was the missing link in my teaching. I had never viewed myself as a writer. Through the workshop experience, I began to view myself as a writer, and that one discovery would change my classroom forever.

When I began teaching third grade, unlike previous years, old fears of teaching writing did not surface. I had confidence in myself as a writer and in my abilities to be a teacher of the writer. I knew that my third graders would become writers. I was not afraid of the new challenge.

## Writers' Workshop with Third Graders

Third graders are a unique age, generally between eight and nine years old. They love to talk and share but continue to need reassurance and approval from their teacher. When introduced to the concept of writers' workshop, my third graders were enthusiastic and eager; inhibitions were few. These children felt comfortable with themselves and with one another. They wrote willingly and shared eagerly.

Throughout my years of struggles, trials, and successes with teaching writing to various age levels, I discovered my desire for students to write remained constant, but my method of instruction changed with each new grade level. How I presented writing appeared to be the key, and how I established the writing environment was the most important factor to acceptance and growth. I felt strongly about the concept of ownership and its role in the establishment of an effective writing environment. Ownership is the knowledge children have that writing belongs to them. It is accepting responsibility for ideas written and published. Ownership comes from an environment of acceptance, responsibility, community, choice, and freedom. When ownership is evident, writing flourishes.

One of the most effective ways I have found to promote ownership is through topic selection. Children need freedom to choose their own topics. But, like me, they may be fearful of the freedom offered them. Freedom comes from the understanding that a writer has choices to make. It comes from the knowledge that they can think for themselves and make decisions that are beneficial to them. In order to gain this knowledge, children must be *taught* how to make choices and decisions. Therefore, I teach children how to look at their surroundings, keep lists, make notes of significant occurrences in their lives and in the lives of others, and remember experiences in their past. By modeling children's literature, reflecting on my life, and sharing my own stories, children are shown how to think about things that happen in their lives—things that have meaning to them. As they become more adept at viewing their lives as significant, children begin to see writing as their own; writing that comes from the choices they make that are meaningful to them.

Teaching children to find meaning in their lives is enhanced through the use of children's literature. It has the power to impact and change lives. I use children's literature to spark ideas for writing—books that will somehow touch children's lives. I use Mem Fox's story *Wilford Gordon McDonald Partridge,* as well as Cynthia Rylant's book *The Relatives Came,* because both books deal with memories. As we read about others' memories, we talk about our own and share with one another. Books such as *I Will Always Love You* by Hans Wilhelm and *Chrysanthemum* by Kevin Henkes are also used because children can relate to the characters' experiences (see Appendix 15). Once these books are read, children are encouraged to talk and share similar stories. Finally, they are invited to write.

Author studies further encourage children to find meaning in their lives. Many authors write about their own lives or about situations that occur around them. Patricia Pollaco writes about experiences in her youth in *My Rotten Red-Headed Older Brother* and *My Ol' Man.* Children are encouraged to examine their own lives when they see authors as real people with real lives (see Appendix 15).

Writing with third graders is a joy as well as a challenge. They are full of stories to tell and ideas to share. Writers' workshop has allowed my third graders to grow as writers and as readers.

## Making Writers' Workshop My Own

Because of my success with writers' workshop in the upper grades I followed the same model with third graders. *In The Middle* (Atwell, 1987) served as my resource guide, but over the years I adapted it to fit my own style of teaching and my children's needs. The physical setting of my classroom is structured to include areas for children to conference, an area for teacher–student conferences, a place for group share, a publishing center, and secluded areas for students to write. There are five key elements that make writers' workshop successful for me. These include uninterrupted times to write, time to conference, time to share, time to self-evaluate, and time for the teacher to write and share. A schedule is developed whereby students are engaged in writers' workshop for one hour each day.

**TABLE 4.1** **Daily Schedule**

|  | Monday | Tuesday | Wednesday | Thursday | Friday |
|---|---|---|---|---|---|
| 8:15 | Mini-lesson | Mini-lesson | Mini-lesson | Mini-lesson | Mini-lesson |
| 8:30 | Writing | Writing | Writing | Writing | Writing |
|  | Teacher conference | Teacher observation | Teacher conference | Teacher observation | Skills groups |
| 9:00 | Silent writing |  | Silent writing |  |  |
| 9:15 |  | Group share |  |  | Author's chair |

### Time to Learn

The majority of our workshop time is spent in student writing. Simply telling children to write for thirty minutes each day, however, is not enough to improve writing. Specific instruction must occur. Children must be shown and taught the skills and crafts that make for better writing. Therefore, the hour begins with a mini-lesson, which takes place within the first five to fifteen minutes of the workshop. During this time, I teach lessons that will help children improve upon their writing. I have adapted Atwell's (1987) three types of mini-lessons, which include procedural lessons to teach the logistics of the workshop, skill lessons to teach grammar and spelling, and craft lessons to teach literary elements. Procedural lessons are primarily taught at the beginning of the year in order to structure the environment and decide upon rules of the workshop. The rest of the year is spent with the skills and crafts necessary to become more proficient writers. These lessons are taught not in a specific sequence but as the children need them in their writing.

Children's literature is used to teach the process, skills, concepts, and literary elements of writing (see Appendices 3 and 4). I use books to demonstrate various skills such as how to set appropriate paragraphs or how to use quotation marks in conversations. Through the use of literature, I am able to demonstrate effective writing techniques. Children are shown how different authors deal with descriptive language, paragraph structure, effective leads, punctuation, and so forth. These books are made available throughout the workshop and serve as reference guides for the children.

Time to learn is a necessity that offers stability to the workshop. Children come to depend on the lessons taught and begin to use the newfound skills and crafts in their writing.

### Time to Write

During writers' workshop children spend the majority of their time writing. They need a sustained period of time in which to write, conference, and think. During writing time children are at various stages of the writing process. Some are drafting and some are ready to revise, edit, or publish. In addition, children are located at different places throughout the room. There are children at the computer typing their stories, pairs of children conferencing in corners, and others who are working with me. As a facilitator of the writing process, I must be aware of where each child is in the process as well as alert to what is going on in the room at all times. I need to be aware of how children are progressing, aware of potential difficulties or inappropriate patterns developing. I must be aware of children who conference all the time, write very little, struggle with topic selection, and believe their first draft is their finished piece. These are the children who need my guidance. My job is to help children progress in their writing. In order to do that I must know where children are and how to help them move forward. I call this awareness "with-it-ness." It is the ability to maintain structure and order, follow each child's growth, and keep the flow of the workshop going. I do this by making observations, asking questions, and keeping accurate notes. It is the notes and anecdotal records I keep that allow me to make appropriate decisions about individual and group instruction.

### Time to Talk

Conferences are a major part of the writing time. While I want children to spend time writing, I also understand the importance of talk as it relates to writing. Students engage in two types of conferences in my workshop. These are teacher–student conferences and peer conferences. The teacher-student conference is an uninterrupted time for a student and the teacher to discuss the story and any problems encountered. I make note of the successes, growth, and areas where the author needs assistance. Feedback and suggestions are given.

The peer conference takes place as two students sit together and discuss their writing. They are given between five and ten minutes. A timer is set and when the bell rings the next pair moves to a conference area. Conferences are a time for students to make suggestions, offer feedback, and encourage and learn from one another. While third graders are talkative by nature, this type of talk does not come naturally to them. They must be taught how to conference with each other effectively. In order to do this, I model an effective and ineffective conference and involve students in role playing. Students watch as I model appropriate questions and useful feedback. They are then called upon to role play with me and then with each other. In this way I can observe how well children are grasping the idea, make note of where problem areas are, and provide practice in the art of conferencing.

When children are first learning how to conference, their comments and feedback tend to be general. For example, one day while role playing, Anna, upon hearing the ending of Katie's story, responded with, "It was good." While telling someone their story is good is certainly not damaging, it is an ineffective response to give to a child's written work. I asked my students, "What does *good* tell you?" I explained to them the term *good* tells us very little and gives no concrete feedback about the story. I further instructed them to be specific in what they liked and ask questions in order to clear up confusing passages.

As children gain more experience with conferences we brainstorm types of questions that would be helpful to ask; questions such as:

"Does my title hook you in?"
"Is my story too long?"
"Does my lead need to be changed?"

Through brainstorming, students begin to internalize the types of questions that should be asked.

*Taliaha asks for help from Morgan during a peer conference.*

Twice a week a group share time is held at the end of writers' workshop. This allows students to receive help from the group. Students are able to read their pieces and receive feedback from the entire group instead of only one, as in peer conferences. In addition to help received, group share also encourages children to celebrate their writings and accomplishments. It is an opportunity for self-esteem to grow as children are positively affirmed in their writings.

*Kyle asks for help from the entire class during group share.*

There are guidelines that must be followed during group share. Students requesting the conference must tell their audience what they need help with. Once the story is read, consideration of the author's feelings is a must. Therefore, students are instructed to say something positive about the writing first and then ask a question or give constructive suggestions for improvement. I model this procedure as I read my story. I begin by saying, "I need you to listen in order to determine if my plot is clear." Or, "What do I need to add to my story to make it more interesting?" Once the story is read, children give me feedback to the questions I posed. These demonstrations teach students to help others and clarify their own writing. As more experience is gained, I am impressed by the higher-order thinking the students use as they critique their classmates' works. They begin to analyze and evaluate writing as to its effect on an audience. The feedback given is then used by the author to revise and edit.

Group share is a vital element of writers' workshop. This was made evident to me one day toward the end of my second year with third graders. I had noticed my students appeared to be in a slump about their writing. They were having difficulty finding topics, completing drafts, and engaging in any revision. After observations and reflections on what was happening, I realized I was not allowing the class to share. We had gotten out of the habit of sharing twice a week, and it was showing. We once again began our regularly scheduled group share. Children seemed to come alive. They stimulated one another to think of sequels to write and new ideas on which to focus. I had learned a valuable lesson. Children must be given time to share.

### Time to Self-Evaluate

At the beginning of each workshop, students set goals for the day. They decide on what they will work on and how much they wish to accomplish during the hour. Goal setting helps children focus and stay on task. It is a way to assist children in learning to become self-evaluators. Responsibility occurs as they set goals and determine whether or not the goals are met.

Writers' workshop ends with self-evaluation. This is the time students reflect on the workshop—the goals set and accomplishments made. Self-evaluation is imperative. It encourages responsibility for one's own learning and holds each student accountable. In my writers' workshop, I want students to evaluate themselves with regard to task performance: Did I accomplish what I set out to accomplish today? They do this in the form of a plus, a check, or a minus. A "plus" indicates that a student stayed on task the entire hour and accomplished the goals set at the beginning of the day. A "check" identifies the student who was off task at some point but still completed some writing. For a student who accomplished very little, a "minus" is given.

I have found over the years that self-evaluation is a new concept for students. They have rarely been given the opportunity to reflect on their own performance. To demonstrate the process, I lead them through the first self-evaluation by beginning the conversation:

> *Teacher:* David, what is your assessment of your performance in writers' workshop today?
> *Student:* I think I deserved a check today.
> *Teacher:* Why do you think you earned a check?
> *Student:* I wrote some, but then I became stuck.
> *Teacher:* What did you do when you became stuck?
> *Student:* First, I drew a picture, then I conferenced with a friend.
> *Teacher:* Look at the chart on the wall about ideas to do when you are stuck. One of the ideas is to draw and another is to ask for help. You did exactly what you should have done. I think you deserve a plus. Is it O.K. if I give you a plus for today?

Until this process becomes more routine, I continue to question and help students understand the concepts of reflection and self-evaluation (see Appendices 5, 6, and 7).

Writers' workshop provides time for instruction, learning, talking, evaluating, and writing. It is only with time and patience that the components of the workshop come together for the benefit of young writers.

## Challenges I Face

Throughout my seven-year journey of using writers' workshop, I have met with several obstacles. There are two, however, that caused me immense frustration—instruction of skills and organization of time.

### Mini-Lessons

When I began writers' workshop, I established a structure and routine that worked for me. I began each day with a mini-lesson. What appeared on the surface as a relatively easy task to accomplish actually became a challenge to overcome. The management of mini-lessons, as well as planning appropriate lessons that would meet the needs of all children, was difficult.

The topics chosen for the mini-lessons were based on skills and writing techniques I noticed the children needed. For example, my children became users of conversation early in their writing and needed assistance on the fine art of quotation marks. I planned a lesson on the rules of quotation marks using a piece of children's literature to serve as a model. I discovered that one lesson on the rules of conversation, however, was not enough. Third graders needed repetition. They needed to be shown over and over the appropriate use of quotation marks, and they needed time to assimilate the information in order to use it in their writing. My struggle came about in planning multiple lessons on the same skill. I had difficulty developing lessons that would interest children as well as teach them the necessary skill. I could come up with one lesson, but two or three? I was at a loss.

Even today, I continue to struggle with the development of multiple lessons on one topic. I want my lessons to be stimulating and creative. But I have come to learn over the years that every lesson cannot be as creative as I would like it to be. My goal is to instruct children on techniques that will assist them in their writing. Some will be creative; some will not. I constantly search for innovative ways to teach mundane rules and procedures. Sometimes, however, I find that simply telling children the rule, putting that rule on chart paper, and focusing their attention on it is enough. I continue to learn that teaching is not about being creative and "cute." It is about relevancy in student learning. Teaching rules and techniques of writing is no different.

Although teaching multiple lessons on the same topic was a concern, planning appropriate lessons to meet all children's needs was a bigger challenge. While most children benefited from lessons on quotation marks, other topics were less generalizable to the entire class. For example, some children needed direct instruction on the use of end punctuation, while others did not. I had difficulty deciding to whom I should teach certain skills, when to teach those skills, and how much time to spend on them.

I knew instruction was important, but how to disseminate the information in a timely, appropriate manner baffled me. I first tried following the sequence in my English book. I planned short lessons that followed a sequence laid out by someone else. It worked by keeping me focused on skills that needed to be taught, but it took away the need that the children had. I then tried keeping a running list of skills taught. This, at least, gave me a record of topics covered. It still did not help me in assisting some children and prevent me from boring other children who already had a grasp of the topic.

I became so frustrated on one occasion that I went to my students. I told them of my struggle to plan lessons that would be beneficial to them and help improve their writing. I finally asked my students what they needed help with. I was surprised at the responses and the lack of hesitation on their part:

> "I need help knowing when to start a new paragraph."
> "How do you know where to put the marks that show someone is talking?"
> "Could you show me how to make my ending better?"

I could not believe the comments my students made. The students knew what they needed and what they did not. I learned a valuable lesson that day. I learned to talk to my students and listen to what they had to say. Children know what they need if we only give them the opportunity to tell us.

Although my students knew what they needed, it still did not solve the problem of who needed what and when. I looked to Calkins (1994) and Atwell (1987) for advice. Both authors discuss the use of skills groups. I had scheduled these groups into my workshop, but had never really used them to their fullest potential. Skills groups allow a small number of students to come together with the teacher in order to receive more in-depth instruction and practice on particular areas of need. I slowly began incorporating these groups into my weekly schedule. I made notes of areas of need as I conferenced with individual children and as I walked around the room. When I noticed more than one child in need of work on a certain skill, I called these children together. We spent time discussing the topic, giving examples, and practicing in our own writing. In utilizing these small groups I was able to focus on specific children who needed help without boring other children who did not. Finding time to include these skills groups in my writing workshop continues to be a challenge. I have seen the advantages, however, and will continue to find time for them.

Once I began to find solutions for what to teach and how to teach it, I was then faced with the organization and management of mini-lessons. I followed Atwell's (1987) suggestion of three types of mini-lessons. I understood the importance of procedural lessons at the beginning of the school year and had little difficulty in designing and including these lessons. It was the craft and skill mini-lessons that challenged me. In order to improve writing, children needed both types of lessons. My problem arose as I tried to organize and schedule the two types of lessons. How could I keep up with the crafts and skills taught? How would I stay organized?

During my first year with third graders I tried to place all my lessons in a plan book. I felt I could come back to this book year after year and remember the basic structure of the lesson and then adapt it to my current group of students. That did not happen. As I began my second year and turned to my plan book, I found there was not enough information to remind me of what I had done. There were books I had used whose titles I could not remember. I knew I had to devise another plan.

After much struggle, I discovered that even though groups of students are different, there are similar skills and crafts that all students need to know. For example, all students need to know when to start a new paragraph, what elements are needed to make a story, what creates interest in a lead, and how to write an effective ending. The lessons may need to be adapted for different groups, but the message remains the same. Once I discovered this, I needed a way to organize my lessons so I could use them from year to year. If there were similar topics that needed to be taught, I wanted a way to preserve the lessons.

I set aside a filing cabinet drawer for my mini-lessons. For each skill or craft I taught, I made a folder. Inside the folder was my lesson plan. The plan was informal but allowed me to use the ideas from year to year. Also inside the folder were the titles of children's literature I used to teach that particular lesson. If a writing sample was used, it went in the folder as well. The next year when the need arose to teach a particular topic, I took out the folder and examined the way it was presented. I then adapted the plan to fit the needs of my current students.

The management of mini-lessons continues to be a challenge. For some teachers, the organization of instruction is an easy matter. They simply follow a textbook and plan direct instruction lessons as they appear in the text. But for those teachers, like me, who follow the needs of their students, organization is difficult. I have begun to find solutions to these problems, and as I move forward and grow with writers' workshop, I keep my eyes open and my mind alert to new methods.

### Finding Time

When I began using writers' workshop, I had just begun to view myself as a writer. I had many fears and inhibitions, but I knew in order to effectively teach my children to write, I had to be a writer myself. When children see me write, they know I value the process. I am able to experience the same kinds of things children do when they write. This gives me insight into their struggles and frustrations. I am able to help them search for solutions and solve problems because I have experienced the same things. In addition, writing for myself provides me with stories to share. I can then use these stories to model effective and ineffective aspects of writing.

When I realized I was no longer able to write during the workshop, I went to the children for help. I explained my concerns and my need to write along with them. Suggestions were given that involved a scheduled time for me to write. Because of the nature of children this age, however, more teacher–student interaction was needed throughout the writing process. I found third graders needed constant reassurance and support. They needed someone to listen to them—someone to give them feedback. At times it seemed as if some child needed my help from the time we began writers' workshop until time for group share at the end.

We finally devised a plan that has continued to work over the years. We now have what I call a sustained silent writing time which takes place twice a week for fifteen minutes. During this time everyone writes with no interruption. It is a time when my students and I write silently. There is no sharing, talking, or conferencing. This gives me the opportunity to write uninterrupted at least twice a week. It also affords children the opportunity to write in silence. While the plan is not foolproof, it has continued to work for me.

Struggles and obstacles are inevitable in writers' workshop. Because the nature of the technique is allowing children to progress at their own pace, there are inherent problems. I have found that stepping back, talking to a trusted colleague, and asking my students for input has had positive effects on the challenges I face.

## Reflections

In anything we do in life, there are positives and there are negatives. There are successes and there are failures. The writers' workshop has allowed me to help children focus on writing for meaning and purposeful use. Students have gone through the process at a natural, realistic pace. Because of this, they have written and enjoyed the excitement which writing affords.

All ability levels have been touched by the use of writers' workshop. All children benefit because of the format that allows them to work at their own level of ability. Children who attend resource classrooms have especially benefited and enjoyed the workshop. During the past year, I had three of these students leave the room for special help during part of writers' workshop. They were devastated to learn they would not get to write. They complained to their parents and the resource teacher, and I eventually changed the time of the workshop to allow these students to participate. These students struggled during other parts of our day, yet because of their success during writing time they wanted to take part in it. Mason was one of those students who made great progress throughout the year. In September, he only wrote a sentence or two while his drawing occupied the biggest part of his writing. By April, Mason was writing full-length stories. He still struggled with invented spelling, but his stories were rich with details. He, like others in the class, had become a writer.

*Mason's writing is mostly drawing in September.*

*By April, Mason is writing longer, more detailed stories with very few drawings.*

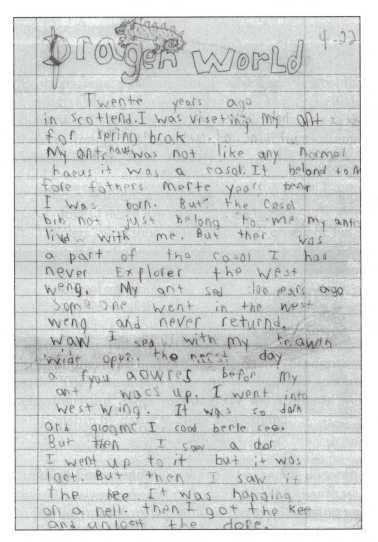

At this point in my career, I cannot imagine teaching writing any other way. I believe in this approach, and I have seen the success it creates in elementary students. I still do not have all the answers. I probably never will. But, through the research and readings of Atwell (1987), Calkins (1994), and Graves (1994), I continue to learn. Through discussions with supportive colleagues and the daily experiences of writing with my students, I have grown immensely as a teacher of the writer. My children and I have learned the joy of writing.

# CHAPTER 5

# Reflections of a Fifth Grade Teacher of the Writer

## Suze Gilbert

*From the time writers' workshop began, Liz never had any problems coming up with topics. She was always eager and ready to write. Liz's pieces generally started out with a bang: catchy lead, detailed accounts, and interesting story lines. Her endings, however, were another matter. Liz seemed to drop the story in the laps of her readers. She built up to this wonderful possibility that never came. In conferences, Liz and I had many conversations about revising her endings. We made reference to books and other students' writing. We examined the way authors end their stories. Liz couldn't grasp this idea. I became frustrated and was ready to write her endings for her when one day she came to me beaming. "Mrs. Gilbert, you have to read the new ending to my story about Grandpa Joe!" Liz said. I could see the excitement in her eyes as I asked what I was to look for in the new ending. Liz beamed while she told me she finally created an ending that her reader could see and feel instead of just "read." I too was thrilled as Liz shared her ending with me. Truly it had come alive, and I soon felt Liz's accomplishment and the excitement that came with it.*

Once again, one of my young writers had taught me a valuable lesson and reconfirmed my belief in the process of teaching writing: students must be given the time to digest the lessons presented to them in the workshop. They must be given ownership of their works and the freedom to fail as they work within the process of writing. This lesson has become the foundation of my writers' workshop.

## My Evolution as a Teacher of the Writer

My evolution as a teacher of the writer began with my first school experiences. The only writing I remember being involved in during elementary school is the dreaded "What I Did on My Summer Vacation" stories assigned at the beginning of the term. The stories were the same each year, bland sentences about the trips I took and the things I did to occupy my time during those summer months. Writing was not emphasized throughout the remainder of the school year. "English" was the emphasis. Day after day I spent time memorizing grammar rules, parts of speech, and identification. When I moved from elementary school to high school, composition classes became the focus. Memories of the "summer vacation" stories written in elementary school returned as I was assigned a topic, a length, a set number of sources to use, and, of course, a due date. As with most students, I waited until the last minute to write the paper and dreaded having it returned. When, weeks later, I did receive my writing, it either had red marks all over it or it simply had a letter grade on it. What did I learn from this? I learned there were seven deadly sins of writing and committing those sins was costly for the grade. Most significantly, I learned I wasn't a writer.

As a college student I learned in my language arts classes that there was more to the teaching of "English" than grammar and parts of speech as I had been taught. I was introduced to the teaching of writing, which meant motivating students to write through the use of story starters. I learned that story starters were the way to promote student writing. Nothing was ever mentioned about choice and student ownership.

When I began teaching fifth grade I taught "English" very traditionally. I followed the basal textbook, lecturing on each part of speech or mechanics rule. Students would then complete the exercises. I devoted one day per week to writing. On these writing days I provided the students with a story starter of my choosing and left them to the task. I was extremely frustrated with the way in which I was teaching English. I hated the textbook, and the students halfheartedly wrote the sentences and underlined nouns or verbs or whatever the directions demanded. In addition, I quickly learned that children weren't any more enthusiastic about writing than I had been. There seemed to be no connection between what we were covering in "English" and what the students were doing with their writing. Students may have scored high on the tests and skill exercises, but their writing was still substandard. It took only one year of teaching for me to start thinking, "My students can't write." Along with this thought I began asking the following questions: "How can I get my students to be enthusiastic about writing?" "How can I turn them into writers?"

During my second year of teaching, I began working on my master's degree. In both the reading and language arts classes I took, the catch-phrase was "whole language." The whole language philosophy was described as a belief that children become literate through the use of real literature and through the use of their own experiences and interests (Bergeron, 1990). A lightbulb went off for me. I realized the importance of literacy to my children's lives. Being literate is important to all people, and learning to read and write is a process that must be experienced by each individual learner. Becoming literate must include freedom, control, and ownership on the part of the learner so that individual interests and aptitude can be nourished. I concluded that my frustrations with teaching language arts, as well as my students' frustrations, stemmed from the inconsistencies between the way I was teaching and the natural way in which children become readers and writers.

Slowly I began to view myself as a holistic teacher. I continued to read and reflect on my beliefs as they related to teaching and learning. My belief system was becoming firm; yet I was unable to nail down a workable plan for classroom practice until I was introduced to the book *In the Middle* by Nancie Atwell (1987). As I read about readers' and writers' workshop, I was hooked before I finished the book. I believed the workshop approach fit with the beliefs I now held about teaching and learning. I dove in the very next August, determined to have writers and readers leave my classroom by the end of that school year.

I no longer used story starters or relied on the textbook for lessons. Instead, I allowed students to own and control their writing by letting them choose their own topics. I used real children's literature to teach lessons on skills and techniques for better writing. I chose lessons based on the needs of my students. Since that first year, I have done much evaluating, questioning, and reflecting in order to determine what is behind the writers' workshop and why I believe in it.

What I've come to believe is that children come to us as writers. We are all writers. We are born with a need to be heard, to tell our story. Unfortunately, what we have done in our schools is take away the opportunity and reasons for children to tell their stories and to be heard. How can we expect children to tell wonderful stories when we assign them to write about their summer vacations? How can we expect them to use vivid language and correct punctuation if the only time they practice is on meaningless sentences in a textbook? For writing to become meaningful and natural for children, it must become personal and interpersonal. We must allow our students to own their writing by giving them time and freedom to move through the process at their own pace and in their own way. Children must be given the opportunity to put on paper the stories they naturally want to tell. I believe that children benefit from time to conference and learn from each other. It is necessary for our classrooms to become strong communities of learners where students are free to express their thoughts and feel safe to hear what others think. We as teachers must show them how to share their stories more beautifully. The teacher becomes a facilitator of learning while the students' needs direct the decisions we make. Only when children take ownership and responsibility for their writing will they truly become writers.

## As It Works for Me

It has always been important for me to remember that there is no right or wrong way to conduct the writers' workshop. In addition, it has been meaningful to reflect upon and base my actions on the beliefs and underlying philosophy supporting the workshop. With each reflection, the workshop itself grows and changes as I learn new things about how children learn the process of writing.

Following the lead of Nancie Atwell (1987) and Lucy Calkins (1986), my workshop is always a predictable environment. Each class begins with a fifteen- to twenty-minute mini-lesson. This is the time I set aside for whole group instruction on skills or crafts from which I feel all of the students can benefit. I use this time to go over grammar rules, mechanics, punctuation, literary devices, and the basic tools that writers employ to make their writing the best that it can be. I try to choose lessons that are timely, meaning that the students can benefit from that lesson when it is given. It is also important for me to incorporate real children's literature as much as possible. For example, Jane Yolen's *Owl Moon* is full of similes and metaphors. When my students are ready for a formal lesson on this literary device, I share the book, and we discuss Yolen's use of simile and metaphor (see Appendix 4). The students are then encouraged to find places where similes and metaphors can make their own writing more meaningful (see Appendix 15).

Immediately following the mini-lesson, I do "status of the class" (Atwell, 1987, p. 91). This is the time I ask each student to identify what he or she plans to work on that day. I quickly jot down what they tell me on a weekly chart. Because each student is in a different place in the writing process, it is important for me to have a record of where they are and what they are doing. I later use this information to assist me in planning lessons, scheduling conferences, and evaluating progress. It also allows me to show parents or administrators what each student is involved in on a daily basis.

The bulk of the workshop time is spent in actual writing. This is the time when students write, conference, revise, edit, and do all the things writers do. Both the students and I are busy and active during this time. I conduct small-group lessons, individual conversations, and editing conferences. The students are involved in a variety of activities; some are drafting, some are conferencing, some are editing, and others are working on final copies. There is a buzz of activity during this twenty-five- to thirty-minute block of time.

The workshop ends each day with a share session. This is a time for children to share their work and ask questions of the whole community. I have found that time is a factor here. There is not always enough of it. I have remedied this situation by having my students focus on a particular topic or problem rather than simply reading their entire piece to the group. In this way, children receive necessary help and support from one another.

I think it is important to repeat that there is no one way to use writers' workshop. The key is to make it work for you and your students. It has been very helpful for me to reflect on the workshop each day, to ask myself what things are working and what things are not, to examine my strengths as a teacher of the writer, and to applaud my own successes as well as those of my students. This reflection has helped me confirm my beliefs in what I am doing. It has helped me grow with the workshop.

## Climbing the Hurdles

Although I have met with many successes throughout the years, any teaching strategy, method, or philosophy is not without its obstacles. The writers' workshop is no exception. My workshop has undergone changes each year as I determine areas of struggle or frustration within my students and/or me. I no longer use the English textbook as my instructional tool or the students' practice manual. Therefore, I have struggled with wondering whether or not they are actually acquiring the necessary grammar and mechanics skills. I have learned, however, to look for evidence of students' learning in their writing. I have also struggled with my evaluation practices. It has been difficult to meet my school system's requirements of grades while remaining true to my belief that children's writing cannot be controlled by grades. I have come to understand there are several ways to evaluate students' writing and grammar skills. I have learned to take daily notes on individual students. I look for areas of strengths and weaknesses. In addition, I use rubrics and checklists to assist me with evaluation. I also provide students with the opportunity and time to evaluate themselves and their writing.

Although I have struggled with accountability and evaluation, it is within the writing process that my greatest frustration has occurred. The first phase of the writing process has been referred to as topic searching, prewriting, and rehearsal. Through my reflection and experience, this phase has come to mean a place where writers decide on and develop a topic. Rehearsal is vital in the process of writing. It is here that many of the major decisions of writing are made. Students choose a genre in which to write. They map and plan the characters, the setting, and the basic plot of the story. I have found that rehearsal is frequently deleted from the writing process. Students do not or cannot take the time to engage in the development of topics. Therefore, their writing is bland and uninteresting.

Because of my limited knowledge of rehearsal and its importance, I began the first several years by allowing and even encouraging students to begin drafting on the first day of the writers' workshop. I told them they could write about anything they wanted as long as it was a story they wanted to tell. Over the next few weeks I introduced, through mini-lessons, the stages of the writing process—the first being rehearsal. Lessons centered around topic selection, as this was what I knew rehearsal to be at that time. I discussed brainstorming and other techniques that would help students generate topics. This was frustrating to many of my students and made little sense because they were already drafting—they had already focused on a topic. I was doing lessons on the first stage of the writing process, but I had already moved them to the second stage.

While some students were very content to begin drafting, others sat and stared at the blank page as if they were waiting for divine inspiration. Often this went on for several days. During this time, I engaged these students in one-on-one conferences and asked questions that could possibly direct them toward a topic. I became very frustrated, as did the students. They simply could not come up with anything they wanted to write. I recalled my college days and my first years teaching language arts when story starters were the key, but assigning a topic would be in direct opposition to the ownership goal of the workshop.

For the first years of the workshop, I simply accepted the fact that some students could not come up with a topic. When the deadlines grew closer I pushed these students harder and, in my frustration, I simply left them alone to complete the task as best they could. Eventually they wrote about something that they were obviously not deeply involved in—a piece just to meet the deadline. I edited the writing with dread because the pieces were undeveloped, often covering several topics.

Even with all my efforts, I could not seem to help these students. My conferencing questions weren't working, and, amazingly, divine inspiration was failing the students as well. I was unable to help my students become deeply involved with their topics. For a time, I tried telling myself that some students simply could not write; they just could not or would not learn the process. They were too lazy to develop a topic or even come up with one. Of course, all the reading and reflecting I was doing was telling me this was not true. In fact, all children could write, and given the right tools they would.

Four years after I had begun implementing writers' workshop, a colleague attended an International Reading Association conference. She loaned me a book she had come across, *Time for Meaning* by Randy Bomer (1995). The book was written by a junior high school teacher who used the writers' workshop approach to teach language arts. He discussed his use of writer's notebooks and what a difference they had made with his students. Bomer devoted several class sessions to teaching his students how to use the writers' notebooks. He modeled techniques such as memory writing, observations, and freewrites. He helped his students share their entries in small and large groups. Bomer found the use of writer's notebooks helped ease his students into the writers' workshop.

I was familiar with journals before reading *Time for Meaning* and had always required my students to purchase one. I had encouraged them to carry their journals wherever they went and make notes of things they observed, things they felt, or things they remembered. I discussed the idea of using the journal to help in developing topics. Some students did this and they loved the idea of keeping a journal. Others hated it and they struggled as much with things to put in their journal as they did with finding a topic. After reading *Time for Meaning*, I realized I was leaving students to the task of using their journals with no real instruction concerning the value of them. I was not making a connection between the journals and true rehearsal.

Rehearsal involves coming to view the world and everything around us as potential for writing. The following year, I began writers' workshop with a focus on that concept of rehearsal. I made use of the writer's notebook as a tool in this endeavor. Writers' workshop began with a brief overview. The writer's notebook then became the focal point of our discussions. We discussed what a writer's notebook looked like and where one could be purchased. It has always been important for me to write with my students during writers' workshop. Therefore, I purchased a notebook and shared it with my students. I explained why I had chosen this particular notebook with angels on the cover. The notebook would become a place for my own personal journey through writing. I wanted my notebook to be an extension of who I was. I felt that by sharing my writer's notebook with the students, I could demonstrate that I would be an active participant in the workshop. I believe students should be allowed to choose their own notebooks, thus contributing to the element of ownership and enhancing positive attitudes about the process. Therefore, I did not purchase notebooks for my students. They were given one week in which to purchase notebooks that had special meaning to them.

Once notebooks had been purchased, I explained the difference between a writer's notebook and a diary or journal. A journal or diary is a recounting of daily events, whereas a notebook is a place to record reflections, thoughts, feelings, and observations. Our writer's notebooks, therefore, became places to play with our writing, search topics, and experience revisions. Later, when we began drafting, the writer's notebook would continue to be a valuable tool for each of us.

Strategies for using the writer's notebooks were introduced through mini-lessons. I did not tell the students to look for a topic—"finding a topic" was not the issue. I wanted them to become comfortable with simply writing. I wanted my students to "feel" writing in everything they saw and did. Therefore, mini-lessons focused on different techniques that would help them come to live the life of a writer. Among other things, I taught students how to engage in freewrites, record observations, reflect on their thinking, and explore memories. Once a particular technique had been explained and modeled, students spent their writing time using the technique. We then shared what we had written.

I found this method not only provided valuable instruction about rehearsal, but it also allowed my class to grow together as a community. We were learning about each other through the notebooks, and we were coming to trust each other by sharing our writings in a safe environment. The students enjoyed writing in their notebooks during class and sharing their work. I had never seen a group so fired up about writers' workshop so quickly in the school year. As I think back on that first year of using writer's notebooks, I believe the students felt more comfortable with their writing. I was no longer throwing them out there to start working immediately through a process they did not understand. Rather, I was taking them slowly through the first and most important phase of the process. Rehearsal allowed the students to discover that they were writers, that writing did not always have to be formal, and that writing does take place outside the four walls of the classroom. I also found that when I began requiring them to use their writer's notebooks outside of class, it wasn't such a big deal to them. The notebooks had meaning and purpose and they loved using them.

I spend approximately six weeks emphasizing and practicing techniques with the writer's notebooks. With the knowledge of living the life of a writer, I feel students are then ready to begin drafting. To begin the drafting phase, I tell my students that we are looking through our writer's notebooks searching for possible themes that may be present. I demonstrate with my notebook by looking for events, people, feelings, or memories that I have written about several times. These entries are placed on transparencies and shared with the class. I demonstrate how I have discovered themes from my entries. The things that are revisited in my notebook seem to have special significance to me. They have a personal meaning that I can further develop. Once I demonstrate, I invite my students to search their notebooks for common themes. We usually spend four to five days searching our writer's notebooks and sharing with one another the themes we discover.

Once the majority of the students have a working topic, mini-lessons focus on the use of writer's notebooks as planning tools throughout the remainder of the writing process. It is here that the notebooks take on a whole new meaning. Previously, the notebooks were used to write memories, observations, freewrites, or descriptions. Now they would be used to plan drafts, to create a road map in order to help writers focus on that single topic. The notebook would follow the writer through the remaining phases of the writing process.

Mini-lessons, at this point, deal with brainstorming about characters, setting, and events. We discuss using our notebooks to guide us. They become the testing ground for ideas, leads, descriptions, feelings, and so forth. As drafting and revising are taking place, students are free to move back into rehearsal at any time. The writer's notebook allows for this easy transition. The students know that if they become stuck and unsure of where their piece is going, they can turn to their notebooks and test possibilities.

The use of the writer's notebooks made a difference in my workshop. I found that the transition from rehearsal into drafting was much smoother. There was no longer that anxious period without a topic; students no longer stared at a blank piece of paper. The students learned from the very beginning of the workshop that the writer's notebook was a tool they would continuously use and depend on. I also saw a difference in the way students bonded together. Our community gelled quickly and tightly. We were sharing parts of ourselves that were very personal, and we were learning that others had similar experiences, dreams, and feelings. We learned that it was safe to put these things on paper and share them with a community we trusted.

I was amazed at the difference in my students' ability to write. I was no longer editing those short, meaningless personal narratives like I had done before. Writer's notebooks allowed students the time they needed to rehearse, draft, and revise. In addition, the notebooks allowed me the time to observe my students and give them freedom to write at their own pace and in their own way. Students began developing their pieces—pieces that had meaning and substance.

## Reflections That Help Me Grow

As I reflect over the years of my teaching career, I cannot imagine returning to the time before I used writers' workshop. I believe that children learn best when they are allowed time, ownership, and responsibility for their learning. The writers' workshop provides my students with an opportunity to grow as writers. Certainly, it has not always been easy and magical for me or my students. What it has been, however, is a tremendous learning and growing experience for me, and for my students as well. The lessons that I have learned through my struggles and successes continue to shape the teacher I am and the one I want to be.

One of the most valuable lessons I have learned is the importance of reflection. It is through reflecting on my experiences that I become a better teacher of the writer. I am able to make connections between my beliefs and my actual classroom practice. Liz was one of the students who benefited from my reflections. My beliefs about allowing children time and ownership clashed with my practice of expecting too much too soon. I was ready to give up on Liz, but through reflection I learned that I must give all students the time they need to digest the information they are receiving. I learned that my students' time frame does not always mesh with my own. By stepping back and giving extra time to Liz, she was able to create an ending to her story of which she could be proud.

A second lesson I have learned involves the structure and the daily workings of the workshop. I have discovered that there is no one way to do the workshop. Atwell (1987), Calkins (1994), and Graves (1994) have been helpful in my evolution as a teacher of the writer. I have used and relied on the techniques reported and demonstrated by these authors. Their explanations and examples gave me a place to begin—a place to feel comfortable and secure. As a teacher of the writer, however, I have had to take these suggestions and find a way to make them work for me and for my students. I have taken what I read and adapted it to my own style of teaching and to my own belief system. This hasn't been easy, but as I make changes and alterations in my workshop, I always keep in mind that the most important thing is that children are writing. Children learn to write by writing (Smith, 1988). Therefore, I must give my students time to write and time to experience the joy of being a writer.

In addition, I have learned that I must let go of my fear. I began my teaching career in a very traditional manner. I was frustrated with my style of teaching, but it was safe. I knew what should be taught, the order it should be taught in, and the type of evaluation that should be used to determine learning. The safety and predictability of these methods were difficult to let go. In addition, I was held accountable for the skills required by state achievement tests. I spent much time and energy being afraid to deviate from the textbook and traditional methods of instruction, even though my philosophy and beliefs about how children learn were in opposition to traditional approaches.

I have learned to let go of my fear and trust that I am doing what is in the best interests of my students. I now look for evidence that my students are learning the skills they need to become better writers. I allow my students' needs to dictate the lessons I teach. I no longer fear that students are not acquiring skills. I see the use of those skills in their writing.

Change is difficult for most people. The workshop is a different approach to teaching language arts. For this reason, collegial support is vital. I need support from my colleagues to help me let go of the fear, to remind me that struggles are worth the effort, and to assist me as I plan. Of course, it is totally unreasonable to expect all of your colleagues to support your efforts, but having even one person whom you can turn to when you struggle or when you succeed is important.

As I talk with teachers who are beginning the workshop, I share with them the importance of team support. At one school I worked with, a group of teachers formed a share time to offer support for one another. They meet once every two weeks just to talk and share their frustrations and successes. I have had the opportunity to sit at their meetings, and I am amazed at the things that are happening. They are building each other up and keeping each other from giving up. They listen to one another and advise one another. By discussing the problems and frustrations of a few, all teachers are able to brainstorm possible solutions. They keep each other focused and dedicated. They reassure each other that what they are doing is the best thing for their students.

A final lesson I want to share is one that I have to relearn periodically. The lesson involves me and my own self-belief. I CAN DO THIS!! If I believe all children are writers and it is my responsibility to tap into that gift, then I must believe I can be a teacher of the writer. It is so easy to lose confidence and go back to traditional methods. Because of this, I have to learn over and over again that I can do this. The lesson comes to me in many ways, and I have taught myself to look for it because this is the lesson that keeps me focused. I see the lesson in the work that my students do, in their attitudes toward writing, and in the general feeling I get when I enter the workshop. When I see the enthusiasm with which my students approach writing, when I hear them grumble when it is time to stop, and when I hear them support each other as writers, I know that I can do this. My hope is that you will learn it as well while you are building your own workshop. I hope, too, that you will remember to learn it again and again. YOU CAN DO THIS!!

# CHAPTER 6

# I Set Out to Prove You Wrong and Discovered the World of Writing

## Tina Robertson

*As Ashley looked at me, her stringy bangs hanging in her oversized eyes, she said with terror, "But I don't know what to write about, and what if you don't like it? What do you want me to write about? I don't have anything. Do we have to do this? I don't like to write!"*

*When Ashley made these statements, I knew exactly how she felt as I too had the same fears and terrors concerning writing. But just as I had been encouraged to grow as a writer, I hoped to encourage Ashley and watch her as her fears turned into pride over a published piece of work.*

## The Journey

My journey with writers' workshop began when I was introduced, by a college professor, to several unfamiliar concepts, including whole language, writer's workshop, integrated learning, and theme teaching. I was, to say the least, inquisitive. I had been teaching for seven years and had never heard of these concepts. I was asked, however, to incorporate one of these innovative approaches into my teaching.

I was first introduced to two techniques that incorporated whole integrated learning and natural authentic writing. Thematic units were described as a way to intentionally integrate knowledge whereby children are given choices and ownership. Like thematic units, writers' workshop was explained as a way to give children control and ownership of their writing. I was encouraged to implement a thematic unit that would include an opportunity for my students to experience writers' workshop. Although I thought this sounded great in theory, to incorporate required skills around one theme, read using trade books, and teach grammar through writing was the dream of a someone who had been away from the "real" classroom for too long.

I spent much time arguing with this professor over the fact that whole language, theme teaching, and writers' workshop might work in the younger elementary grades, but it could not work with sixth graders. It would simply not offer enough structure. I believed that with too much freedom students would view school as a place to play and valuable time would be wasted. I was adamant in my arguments against such a class being successful, as was the professor in her arguments that it would work. So I decided to prove my point and set out to "teach" using the whole language philosophy while incorporating theme teaching and writers' workshop. I knew if I was to make my argument convincing and prove my point I would have to set the class up properly, just like the experts said, and then carry it out with the utmost determination.

We had four weeks of school left before summer break, and I was about to start a unit on World War II. I began reading books and articles concerning theme teaching and writers' workshop. I followed my instructor's advice as well as that of others from my readings and set out to prove my point that whole language, including theme teaching and writing, would not work in a typical sixth grade class. I knew once I had proven to myself and this instructor that sixth graders needed more structure than these methods provided, I could go back to teaching my grammar and reading classes using the basal and textbooks as the majority of teachers did every day.

I read as much as I could about theme teaching and writers' workshop and for the next four weeks my students "studied" World War II. They mapped out what they knew about the war and researched what they did not know. They read books, both fiction and nonfiction, and shared their findings with other members of the class. In addition, writer's workshop gave them the opportunity to write their own stories set in Europe during World War II. At the end of the four-week period my students were able to show me, through presentations, author's celebration, and high test scores, that they had learned more about the war and related events of that time period than I ever would have been able to teach in my regular social studies class. They wrote with an enthusiasm I had never witnessed, and their stories were actually good! My students were suddenly excited about the process of learning. It was at this point I had to admit to myself I had been wrong. Not only did theme teaching encourage inquiry learning and writers' workshop promote improved writing among sixth graders, but they both generated excitement. This excitement encouraged me to offer the same freedom to explore and discover to all my future classes.

It was this single decision that would begin the largest growth spurt in my journey that I had ever experienced in my educational and teaching career. I began slowly concentrating on one innovation before moving on to another. My journey began by focusing attention on the development of writers' workshop. I knew in order to lead my students in authentic learning where they ask questions, search for answers, and write creatively, I would have to do some work of my own. First, I needed to learn how to incorporate the skills and curriculum requirements of the state into my writers' workshop classroom. I also needed to learn how to be more of a guide and resource for my students rather than a lecturer who simply imparted knowledge. With these things in mind, I registered for a summer class on writers' workshop so I could implement it on a full-time basis in the fall.

In the class I was encouraged to become a writer myself. I must admit, I did not embrace this opportunity, as I had never written anything but a research paper in my life, and I did not enjoy the art of writing. Nevertheless, there I was on author's night with my finished book in hand, ready for my turn to share and proud of my simple accomplishment. I had made it. I was ready to begin my own writers' workshop and share with children their sense of accomplishment as they became writers.

## The Struggles

When I began writers' workshop I became an "inquiry based instructor." I had questions and concerns but began to work out solutions, sometimes through trial and error and sometimes through self-evaluation, depending on the question at hand. My concerns were many and varied. How would I obtain grades for the English section of the report card? When would I teach grammar and mechanics? Was I really a competent enough writer to actually lead my students in writing strategies? As I worked in my classroom to solve each of these stumbling blocks it became a time of great growth, not only for my students but also for me as an instructor and as an individual.

### Grammar Instruction versus Writing

One of the first concerns I struggled with was obtaining grades. My school system required that each child be given a number and letter grade at the end of each grading period. "English" was listed as a subject area on report cards. Therefore, a grade had to be given. I had a hard time envisioning where these grades would come from unless I evaluated the students' writing. Everything I had read or been taught said that "grading" students' writing was inappropriate, as it might make them apprehensive about writing. Previously, English time had consisted of teaching a particular part of speech or mechanics rule and students completing the exercises, either in the book or on ditto pages. Grades had, therefore, come from these exercises. If I began using my English period for writing there would be no time for students to do any drill and practice for assessment and grading purposes. This problem alone was a hurdle I had to overcome before I could implement writers' workshop into my class curriculum.

Because I didn't know any upper grade teachers who used writers' workshop, I spoke to several lower grade teachers about what they did to assess writing. They were not required to give a number grade. I read as many articles as I could find, but none seemed to offer any advice that I could use. I finally decided that since I had to give grades and was not comfortable grading students' writing, I would alternate between traditional English classes and writers' workshop. On Tuesday and Thursday, I used the textbook, taught the skill, and graded the related drill and practice pages. The students wrote on Monday, Wednesday, and Friday and were not graded. The next week I reversed this setup and used the text three days and had children write on two.

As I attempted to solve the problem of grades, however, I became aware of a greater problem—that of teaching the rules of grammar. I knew this information was not only required by the state curriculum guides, but the rules would also be assessed when it came time for my students to take achievement tests in the spring. Since 50 percent of my English time would now be allocated to writing, I knew I would not make it through the entire book and, therefore, would be skipping material I felt was important. I could not decide how to incorporate this material into the writing my students would be doing. In my mind, grammar rules and writing were foreign to each other. I now realize that I had never been taught to use the skills of grammar in conjunction with my writing and, therefore, did not see the relevance of one to the other.

I did not work out this dilemma totally to my satisfaction before beginning writers' workshop with my children that first fall, but I decided to go ahead with its implementation. Because of my concern for the "skills," my goal was to see how far I could get in the English book. Two years later I was still at the same place, concentrating on grammar separate from writing and taking the "English" grades from separate lessons.

This method worked wonderfully for me, but my students had a different opinion. They began to ask, "Are we going to write today?" This question alone invoked guilt in me when I had to answer, "No, today we're going to do some work from the book." I had always believed that learning could and should be enjoyable. If my students were eager to write, then I should be doing what I could to incorporate grammar into their writing. This, however, did not come easily to me. I could not mesh the grammar and writing into one lesson easily. I fought with myself over the best way to do this.

It all came together one day as I was reading some of my students' books.

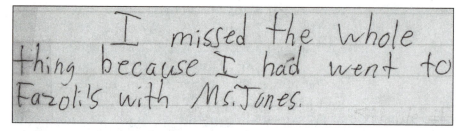

I missed the whole thing because I had went to Fazoli's with Ms. Jones.

While reading Alan Smith's story, I immediately knew that he needed help with the past participles of verbs. I began to plan, and as I did, I wondered where I could get a list of all the words that changed form when they went from past tense to past participle. I reached for my English book to look for the list, and bells went off in my head. All of a sudden I could see where it was possible to tie my grammar lessons into writing. Why didn't I teach several short lessons on the proper use of past tense and past participles of words? Students could then check their writing pieces for any of these types of errors. If necessary, I could ask the students to do a quick ditto for a grade before they began writing one day. I carried the thought a step further; if I taught these lessons and asked the students to check their work for this type of error, why couldn't I hold them accountable for it in their writing? I could either assign small pieces of writing on given topics, which I could assess to determine mastery; or I could assess the writing they were engaged in daily. Either way, I felt it would help my students see the relevance of grammar to their writing and help them see how the two were indeed related.

I sat there amazed at myself. For almost two years I had worried about how to incorporate grammar with writing and make it work. Then all of a sudden the answer jumped out at me. I realized it wasn't the skills that were so hard to tie into writing; it was this teacher's preconceived ideas of what an English lesson should look like and the components it should include. I have since learned to use my English book as a resource tool when I need to teach a grammar lesson. I try to convey to my students that the whole purpose of learning grammar is to better communicate to their audience and thus become more proficient writers. Any rule they may learn from the book is of no use unless it is put into practice in their individual writing and speaking. After all, can you think of another reason to learn grammar rules, unless it would be to become a *Jeopardy* contestant?

Since this realization, I have incorporated every part of my English book into mini-lessons that are taught at the beginning of each writers' workshop. I take ten to fifteen minutes to teach a skill that students need in order to improve their writing. This offers my students the opportunity to write for twenty to thirty minutes a day, five days a week. It has worked well, and students do not seem disturbed by the fact that I now assess their writing. A statement my professor had made two years earlier came back to me: "Make the class your own and make it work for you." I now knew what she had meant. There was not an *exact* way to teach writers' workshop. There was no teacher's manual that suggested a certain way of doing lessons, just as there was no exact way to write a story. Every class would be a little different, just as each story the students wrote would be a little different. I had to find my own way to make writers' workshop fit my style of teaching. With my students' help, I had done that.

## Critical Examinations

Once I realized that grammar could be taught in conjunction with writing, I began to question my ability to design lessons that would teach the strategies necessary to become a better writer. I felt confident in teaching the writing process because it had steps to follow that I could easily explain. I was not at all sure, however, about how to design lessons on subjective items, such as the flow of a story, word usage, pictures with words, adding detail, and removing unrelated items found in stories. This uncertainty caused me to hesitate in my eagerness to incorporate writers' workshop. My hesitancy increased as I questioned my ability to critically examine children's writing for mechanical problems. I had taught the meaning of such things as run-on sentences, sentence fragments, and paragraph structure. To trust myself to find these and other such errors in children's writing, however, was somewhat overwhelming.

At this point in my growth, I had severe self-doubts. I was not confident enough in my own writing skills to believe that I would know how to guide my students to becoming accomplished writers. Nor did I have faith that once my students wrote I could critically evaluate their work and offer lessons that would lead them to becoming more proficient authors. These concerns carried well into my first year of incorporating writers' workshop, but I knew if I allowed my apprehensions to stall my efforts I would never move forward. So I jumped in and began teaching lessons I thought would be helpful.

I began with the writing process since I knew I could follow the outlined stages. I continued looking for answers to my other concerns as well. In so doing, I ran across a book that became very helpful in planning those worrisome strategies and mechanics lessons. *Thinking Like a Writer* by Lou Stanek (1994) was divided into small sections. Each section was designed to teach a lesson that would help students make their writing more interesting and powerful. Along with each short lesson was an activity. I read the lessons to my students, and as a class we did the related activity. The students enjoyed these assignments, and they allowed me the time I needed to become comfortable with reading my students' writing and locating areas in which help was needed. I was also able to get ideas on how to go about setting up strategy lessons that could be beneficial, enjoyable, and meet the needs of growing writers.

The more I taught using the writers' workshop and the more time I spent reading my students' writing, the better I became at locating their areas of need and planning lessons. As with most things in life, the more I worked at being a critical reader of children's writing, the better I became. It wasn't too long before I found myself comfortable reading a piece of writing, commenting on the fine points, and making suggestions on how to improve the areas of need.

With each passing year, planning and implementing writing lessons has become easier. I have saved the overheads and various materials I pull together to teach different writing skills. Each of these lessons is labeled and filed in an orderly fashion; thus, I am quickly able to pull lessons that my students need. For example, if I see that a student's writing does not flow from one idea to the other with clarity, I pull my file marked "bridges." From here I have several different lessons and overheads that I can use to explain and show how authors move from one idea to the next without losing the reader in the process. Included in these files are the names of children's books that demonstrate how authors use language to make their stories more enjoyable. They serve as an aid in helping me teach the particular skill with which I am working.

What amazed me most was the ease with which I went from not trusting myself to being able to identify and correct a student's problem area to actively being able to spot them. All it really took was some practice from the teacher and a group of students who were eager to write.

## Setting the Stage

As I start each year, I have come to realize that many children are much like I was when I began writing. They, too, are fearful and hesitant to travel into uncharted territory. They do not see the tie between writing and grammar, and they are unsure of their own skills as authors.

One of the first concerns students have upon entering my writing class is topic selection. They automatically think they have nothing to write. They have done nothing overly exciting in their lives and do not consider themselves experts in anything. Therefore, they think they have nothing important to share. To keep this from being a stumbling block, I have learned to start my year by reading aloud several short, well-written pieces of children's literature. I spend the first week of school reading various books, including several by Robert Munch. They are entertaining stories written about everyday events that occur in the life of almost every child. My students love them (see Appendix 15).

With these stories the stage is set to introduce personal narratives, which is the first piece of writing I ask my students to participate in. I explain how authors take small pieces of their lives and turn them into entertaining stories. I further explain that this is what they will be asked to do concerning their own lives. Through the books I share, students are given an opportunity to relate published pieces to their own experiences. As they listen to the stories being read, students jot down any words, pictures, or life experiences the books elicit in their minds. They begin to see that they do have things to say. By the end of that first week my students have a list of fifteen to twenty experiences they have related to from these books. I ask them to save this list for later use.

In addition to the read alouds, I have my students list fifty events that have occurred in their lives. The events can be as simple as being stung by a bee to as serious as a surgery they may have undergone. I then ask students to place a star beside ten events they feel have made an impact on the person they have become today. Once they have numbered the events chronologically, I ask students to graph them on a time line. Each event is placed on the year in which it happened and given a vertical position that represents the degree of happiness or sadness it caused. This time line and list of experiences elicited from the literature readings then become ideas my students may pull from as they begin a new piece of writing. Once the students have written stories from these lists and published several books, they begin to grow in confidence. The

*Scarlett's time line*

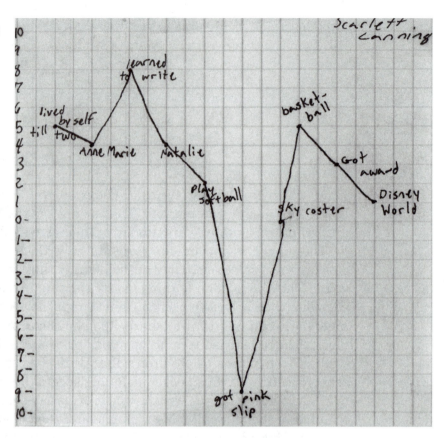

lists are used less and less as the students see more appealing and interesting things around them about which to write.

Once students feel comfortable writing about their lives, I introduce the elements of fiction writing. I explain how authors, many times, will take a fact, expand upon it, and fictionalize it. I then encourage students to take one of the events on their time line and embellish it. They are able to experience the joy of fictionalizing a true event from their own lives. I did not realize how well this worked until at an open house one night a parent brought me his child's writing concerning a hospital visit. He began to explain that the whole book was a fabrication. It seems his son had fallen and received several stitches but was never admitted to the hospital as his book indicated. I was excited to explain to the parent that his child had done exactly what many authors of fiction do: take an actual event and turn it into an interesting story for people to enjoy. I was equally excited to find out that my lessons were indeed hitting their mark. I had read the child's book and thought the whole story to be autobiographical—it was written with such conviction.

The stage is set for writing when students feel a certain degree of confidence in themselves. When they believe themselves to have something worthwhile to say, writing can begin.

# Working Through the Process

### Our First Project

In order to help my students begin their first piece of writing and learn each step of the writing process, I have each choose one event from their time line. Together we go through the process toward writing a personal narrative. We learn rehearsal strategies as well as revision techniques. Students draft and revise as together we learn about the process of writing. For many sixth graders, writing is new. Therefore, the first piece of writing we do together allows me to explain and model each step thoroughly. I then place a detailed step-by-step outline of the writing process on the wall for my students to follow and refer to the remainder of the year. I have found that this outline helps the students stay focused and provides guidance for them throughout the process. This first piece, completed together, also offers me the opportunity to teach my students how to publish a hardback book. As students finish pieces later in the year they may go on to the publishing center I have established. They are then free to publish their own book without interrupting me or the rest of the class.

### Working Together

As I walk my students through this first piece of writing I am able to introduce the idea of peer conferencing. I begin by modeling. I enlist the help of a student who I have prepared beforehand, or another teacher. I am able to demonstrate the steps each conference should follow and introduce the reasons for which conferences should take place. Students are encouraged to conference if they: (1) are stuck as to which direction they want their story to take; (2) want another opinion as to how much detail they need to add or eliminate; (3) want confirmation on the story line they have chosen and need peer support; or (4) need to discuss any aspect of the revising process.

I spend several class periods setting the stage for conferencing and conveying my expectations to my students. In order to keep up with who is conferencing with whom and for what reason, I have students complete a conference sheet each time they meet with a peer. The conference sheet is very basic in that it asks simple questions that will help students focus on the task at hand (see Appendix 9). I keep the conference sheets at my desk, allowing students to obtain them at the beginning of class or in between my conferences with various students. This sheet is then turned in with their finished publication. By requiring this form to be filled out, I am able to pair a writer with a partner who may be slightly more advanced in skills and, therefore, may help the author grow in writing.

This also allows me to quickly monitor how many conferences a child participates in per week. I try to limit a child's conference periods to two a week, whether it is his or her requested conference or one to help a peer. I have found this limitation to be necessary in order to keep some of my more advanced writers from being chosen too frequently. It also limits my reluctant writers from choosing to conference unnecessarily.

The amount of freedom I allow with the conference length, reasons for conferencing, and the selection of peer partners will vary according to the class. If I know the student to be a hard worker who has asked for an extended conference or an additional one, I will determine the problem and pair him with a writer who is strong in that student's particular area of need. By the same token, if I know the child requesting a conference is prone to idleness, I may conference with the student myself in order to motivate and encourage. Once I have a good working knowledge of my class and have observed them over a period of weeks, the issue of conferencing seems to work itself out. Teachers must use their own judgment in this area and trust in their own instincts.

It would be unrealistic to think that no excess talking or visiting goes on during conferences. It does. But, I have noticed as each school year progresses, less and less visiting occurs. By the end of the year many students do not request conferences as often. They begin to see conferencing time as time taken away from writing. Students begin to decline requests to conference with a friend because they want to concentrate on their story and do not want to be interrupted. When this occurs, the child requesting the conference comes to me, and I ask for volunteers to assist. It is encouraging when I see a student decline a conference with a best friend because the student is deep into the story and doesn't want to break a train of thought. This rejection can be hard to accept. If a request for a conference is declined, I caution my students not to become angry but to understand that the author needs time to focus on writing. Working together through peer conferences forces students to assess themselves and determine their own needs. It requires compromise and cooperation.

### Editing: A Critical Look

Conferences are not only used to assist authors while rehearsing, drafting, and revising—they are also used during editing. This phase of the writing process has been a great challenge to me. Because my students believe themselves to be writers, they have a difficult time believing they are capable of making mistakes. They believe it next to impossible to make careless errors like leaving out words or transposing letters. Therefore, there is no reason to proofread and edit their writing once it is complete.

In order to encourage students to take the time to examine their writing critically for editing purposes, I model the importance of it with overhead transparencies. I take exact sentences with visible errors from students' writing. We discuss the errors and why they are a problem. We then examine ways to correct each error. This has proven to be a great technique in teaching my students the capability we all have of making errors in our writing.

When I first began this technique I was skeptical. I worried about using sentences that were exact duplicates of my students' writing as I did not want to embarrass or make anyone feel self-conscious. Many times I found that students did not remember writing the sentence. Who wrote the sentence or paragraph did not seem to be important. The fact that it was a real error that someone in our class had made did seem to hold merit. It appeared that when I showed the students errors they were making, not just some I had made up as examples, it made the lesson more relevant to them. They took the suggestions and applied them more readily.

Once the editing stage has been explained and students are aware of its importance, many rush through it in order to publish. I have tried several different methods to encourage my students to take their time, examine their writing, and edit their books properly. One method that appears to work well for me and my students is an edit sheet. I created this sheet in order to guide my students to look for common errors in their writing. While developing the sheet, I examined grammar and mechanics skills basic to entering sixth graders (see Appendix 12). The sheets are updated throughout the year as we study new rules and skills.

Each student is required to edit the story using the edit sheet as a guide. As they edit, students look for one common error at a time. On the sheet, they initial when they have checked and corrected each error. Once they have checked their own work they pass their book and edit sheet to a peer who checks it for the same basic skills and initials it. Students turn their book in to me for final assessment. When I see blatant mechanical errors that should have been corrected, a postconference is held. At this time I stress the fact that good writers turn in pieces that are as correct as possible in order to lend credibility to their work.

A second approach I have used to encourage my students to edit critically is to have them read their story into a tape recorder. Once the story is recorded, students play it back and listen for inconsistencies between the written and oral reading. Students are better able to locate places where errors have been made. If a student reads a story and still does not recognize careless errors, I have another student read the work into a tape recorder. The author listens to the other student's recording. Reading aloud assists authors in critically reviewing their work.

Finally, I closely monitor students' writing, looking for areas where lessons need to be taught or ways to encourage them to see areas of need independently. For example, when I see my students becoming lax while publishing books, I explore ways I might teach them about self-pride. One thing I have done is make an example book. It contains wrinkled pages, sloppy writing, poor illustrations, and a torn binding. When I ask my students what they see they immediately point out the obvious. We discuss the need for adequate preparation in order to show an audience that authors cherish what they have to say.

Although editing is the final stage a writer goes through, it is no less important than drafting and revision. My goal is to encourage sixth grade writers to look critically at their work in all phases of the process. Editing is no exception.

## The Teacher's Lesson

The lesson of self-pride permeates throughout writers' workshop. As a child takes an idea and turns it into a piece of writing to be shared with others, a sense of accomplishment is experienced by all. This pride is also celebrated by me as I watch my students grow and become more proficient in the art of writing. Throughout the process of incorporating writers' workshop I have learned that a student-centered class, where students are given the freedom to explore their thoughts and build upon them, is a successful class. To plan lessons based on the needs of sixth grade writers takes time and energy. The rewards are worth it. To see the excitement and growth that takes place in the life of one of my students is all the reward I need to continue the journey I have begun.

Ashley, my reluctant writer, showed me the rewards as she approached my desk at the end of the year and remarked: "Mrs. Robertson, how did you like the way I told that story like I wasn't there? It was really my story, but I wanted to tell it like it wasn't me. Did you think that was O.K.?" Ashley was referring to a six-page book she had just finished. This was true progress coming from the student whose first book had been six sentences and who thought she had nothing to write about.

What started as an assignment, one in which I had planned to prove that in the "real world" writing could not be done as a student-centered activity, has grown into a belief far different. I proved to myself that not only could it be done but it could be done in such a way as to make my class an enjoyable place to be while still making a lasting and far-reaching impression on my students.

# CHAPTER 7

# My Journey: Finding the Road with Seventh Graders

## Pat Reneau

*Ashley was self-conscious, as most adolescent girls are during this time in their lives. She did not feel good about herself in anything, personally or academically. Writing, in her eyes, was the second deadliest sin next to reading. She never volunteered to read or discuss any aspect of her writing during group share. When asked a question, she would quickly say, "I don't know," as if to say, "Let me off the hook, please."*

*Most days Ashley was just "there." I watched her during our quiet writing time as she stared into space. Thinking about what she was going to write about, I hoped. When I read her entries, however, they were only attempts at writing words, any words, to prove to me that she was writing. My hope was that she would feel the excitement when others shared. But it didn't happen. She was hard core determined not to write.*

*As the year progressed students began writing poetry. When several of her friends worked on poems, Ashley was sometimes asked to have a conference with one of them. Ashley tried her hand at poetry, and the poems she wrote surprised me. I read them several times and could not hold back my excitement. I immediately had a conference*

*with her. I wanted to grab her, hug her, and
wave the poems in the air shouting to everyone,
"Look, look at these pieces from Ashley! Wait
until you hear how funny they are!" She knew
how proud I was of her; but more importantly,
she recognized pride in herself. Ashley had found
her writing voice.*

Many students, with little or no experience with writing, feel that in order to be a writer they must possess a God-given talent they have yet to receive. These students feel they must begin by writing a masterpiece. Because of these feelings, many young writers are afraid to write. If an attempt is made, it is inevitably compared to others in the class and is usually deemed unacceptable. Ashley's poems were certainly not masterpieces, but they represented her life. Her first poem, "I Wish I Had No Lips," was a result of her summer experiences. She says, "In the summer I would swim. I would be in the sun all day, and my lips would be dry. So I would lick 'em."

*Ashley comes to
believe in herself
as a writer.*

---

I WISH I HAD NO LIPS

Chapped lips, Dried Lips
  Nasty lips
  Red lips

Chapped lips, dried lips
  Scabbed lips
  Bumpy lips

Chapped lips, dried lips
  Soggy lips
  Painful lips

Chapped lips, dried lips
  Amusing lips
  Embarrassed lips

Chapped lips, dried lips
  Unbearable lips
  Freaky lips

Chapped lips, dried lips
  Bad lips
  Sad lips

Poem By Ashley Roth

---

To Ashley, these poems represented an ability to write, something she did not think was possible at the beginning of the year. This is true for many students. They are fearful of the blank sheet of paper; afraid that what they have to say is unimportant and not worth writing. Therefore, I want to instill in them not the necessity of becoming a published writer, but the belief in themselves as writers. I want my students to enjoy writing for the pleasure it can bring them.

## Me?—A Writer?

*I don't have anything to write about! I can't do this! Oh, why am I in this class? This is not what I expected!*

You may be thinking these are the words of those reluctant writers in your classroom. In actuality, however, these were my own words when I encountered a graduate class concerning the teaching of writing. I had been searching for a way to incorporate writing into my language arts block. Therefore, I decided to enroll in a class entitled Writer's Workshop. The school year had started, and my children had already begun to write. I wanted all the information I could get my hands on, and I wanted it right then.

Prior to the beginning of class, the members of the class were asked to purchase journals and begin writing for at least ten minutes each day. There it was! I had enrolled in this class to help me teach my own students how to write. I never dreamed I would actually have to go through the process myself. We were going to learn to teach writing by writing ourselves. Thoughts of panic reverberated inside my head. What had I gotten myself into? *I'll just drop out. But, no, it's too late. I'll just have to struggle through and risk making a fool of myself. I'm an adult. I can handle this.* So, I plunged in.

I remember clearly stating to everyone in the class that I had never really written. Of course I had written papers in college and the ordinary writing that is necessary in a teacher's life. But to write anything creative such as a poem or story? Not I. I, like many of my students, believed I had to create a masterpiece in order to become a writer. I was afraid! Although the fear and panic paralyzed me at the onset, slowly I began to understand myself and my feelings about writing. I began to understand the power of writing. More importantly, I finally understood the feelings and thoughts my students must go through as they write. I worked very hard in that class and wrote two "adult" poems that I am very proud of today. For me, the paths I took and the thoughts that occurred as I wrote were more exciting than the finished product.

Today I continue to write in my journal. Oftentimes I visit it daily to sort through life's struggles, and with this exercise, it helps me find the answers I need. As I write, one topic leads to another and then another, and suddenly I have a great idea for a story or a poem. I find myself seeing a poem or story in everyday observations and everyday thoughts. I tend to examine the writing style of an author when I am reading a novel, something I never did before. I think of writing first now when I'm happy or feeling blue. It's like a chiropractor to my mind. My journal is my life adjuster. I want my students to feel this as well.

I am not saying every teacher who is attempting a writing program with his or her children needs to enroll in a writing class, although it is not a bad idea. I am saying for you to truly understand the frustrations children can have when they write, it is extremely important to write yourself. When they say to you, "I have nothing to write about!" you can better assist them because you know how it feels to have nothing to say. When they say, "How long does it have to be?" you will understand their pressure to perform. There are textbooks that can help you with answers to the questions you will inevitably receive from your students. What better responses, however, than those that are based on your own experiences with writing: "I know how you feel. I feel that sometimes, too, when I write. Let me tell you how I worked through it."

## Beginning My New Journey

When I began my career, I taught reading almost exclusively. After twelve years, I moved to a middle school to begin working in a language arts block, teaching both reading and writing to seventh graders. Because my primary emphasis had always been reading, I had little or no experience in teaching writing. In fact, writing, as an objective, was rarely identified in the curriculum. The occasional essay was assigned with prompts given, and a specified number of words assigned. Writing appeared to be a by-product of grammar and spelling. Many times it served as a "filler activity." The "real" writing did not occur until high school, when students wrote research papers. Process writing was rarely, if ever, taught or practiced.

While I taught second grade, attempts had been made to incorporate writing using animal pictures as a prompt. But, because of my lack of experience, I was nervous as I began teaching the seventh grade language arts block. I was responsible for teaching both reading and writing. Reading came easily for me, but writing was another story. The two subjects were not integrated and very little writing was encouraged other than the three point essay that was required. During my first year, our state had begun the implementation of a writing assessment for eighth graders. I had no idea how to prepare my students. Based on other teachers' comments and my own lack of knowledge, writing instruction was relegated to the teaching of grammar and spelling.

The language arts block consisted of two back-to-back fifty-minute periods. I spent half the time teaching reading and the other half teaching grammar and spelling. I adhered to the state curriculum guides and the trusty English and spelling books. We started at the front of the books and worked our way through the practice exercises. I gave practice sheets on grammar and mechanics for homework and checked them in class the next day. Each day was the same as we moved through lesson after lesson until the unit was finished. Units were then tested, skills not mastered were reviewed, and it was on to the next unit. There were writing activities throughout the English book that we would try from time to time, and extra credit was given if a story was composed with that week's spelling words. Book reviews were written, and I always created essay questions on tests. They were writing, but the writing had been reduced to just another exercise.

The end of the school year was rapidly approaching, and I knew the time had come to teach that elusive three point essay. I taught my students the fine art of writing a three point essay, and they began to spit them out for the remainder of the year. I felt good because my students had learned the grammar and mechanics, and they had actually written. The disappointment, however, during that massive rush to produce three point essays, was in the errors I found in grammar. What had we worked on all year? The skills we had practiced were not being applied in the students' writing. There was no connection being made between any of the language arts.

The language arts block was a wonderful opportunity to help students make connections between and among the language arts. There was so much potential in having a group of students for a large chunk of time. I, along with my colleagues in the language arts department, saw this opportunity, but we had no idea where or how to begin. We needed help. We purchased a copy of Atwell's (1987) *In the Middle* and began reading it along with articles concerned with the reading–writing connection. We discovered that in order for children to grow in reading and writing, they must actually read and write. In addition, we discovered grammar and mechanics were best learned not from practice pages but from real writing. We were totally overwhelmed. More than this, we were concerned about letting go of our English grammar and literature texts. Even though I had seen, firsthand, students who could not apply the skills of grammar to real writing, I was not convinced they would learn anything about the structure of grammar simply by producing pieces of writing. Would they truly be prepared for our state's assessment? Although we wanted change, it seemed as if our curriculum was going to be turned upside down and totally revamped.

Some teachers decided to dive right into the water and began using readers' and writers' workshop, implementing the strategies of Atwell (1987) and the suggestions made by other authors. Some sat on the side of the pool dangling their feet in the water, not quite sure whether to jump in, but willing to try one or two of the strategies in both reading and writing. Some tested the water with only one foot. They either implemented only some of the strategies in reading but not writing or tried some of the ideas in writing while keeping their reading curriculum intact. I jumped into readers' and writers' workshop with both feet. Because of my strong belief in this program, I began my true journey into teaching using the writers' workshop format. Writers' workshop made me feel as if I had truly implemented writing into my curriculum.

## Setting Up the Environment

### Teaching Grammar with No Text

When I began using writers' workshop, I gave up every textbook I had ever used. There were no more grammar exercises from the English book and no more dreaded worksheets. The English books were used for reference only. On the first day of school, I told students we would not use the English and spelling textbooks during Language Arts. I will never forget the expressions on their faces, which, of course, translated into, "Cool, we don't have to do any work in this class." I continued to explain that they would, instead, write, and whatever they wrote would be their choice. Eyes bulged and bodies moved forward in their chairs. They were motionless, breathless, and contrary to the norm of adolescence, speechless. I continued, "The only texts we will use will be your writing journal, writing folders, and writing notes kept in a three-ring notebook." I had their attention, and they were anxious to see how this year was going to fit together.

During the early days, as we began writing, I had some students ask to return to the English and spelling books. These were students who were skill-driven and could not see the purpose in writing. The process of writing was new to them and, for the first time, students were being asked to think for themselves. This left some feeling uncomfortable because of their prior experience with practice exercises where rote memorization was required. Students had a difficult time with the freedom that writers' workshop allowed after years of being told what to write, how many pages to complete, and, in essence, what to think. My environment was somehow unsafe for them. Over time I was able to convince these students that through writing, the skills they learned would be more applicable. At the end of the year students were given a survey concerning their attitudes toward writers' workshop. One of the questions was, "Do you think you know more about using grammar through writers' workshop or by working exclusively in the English book? Why?" Ninety percent of the students said they learned more about grammar through their own writing. Statements that were made include the following:

> "I have learned more about grammar from writing because the mistakes I make are mine, not the book's."
>
> "Writers' workshop makes learning grammar fun. When I do exercises out of the textbook, I don't learn anything because I forget it. When I write a story, I say, 'Oh, I remember that. I used it in one of my stories.'"
>
> "In writers' workshop, we always use what we learn."

The books and articles I had read concerning the relationship between skills and writing had proven to be true. Students were *using* grammar skills. They were learning the structure of grammar as it related to actual writing. More importantly, my students were convinced of this relationship by using writers' workshop.

### Building Community

In the beginning, as we came to terms with using no textbooks and writing instead, *In the Middle* (Atwell, 1987) was my sole reference guide—at least for the first six weeks. It was my Bible and my script. Over time, however, I became discouraged and overwhelmed in trying to incorporate everything in Atwell's book. It was my initial resource in setting up the workshop, but as time went by I began to explore other authorities such as Calkins (1994) and Graves (1994). I also began to look to myself and my own sense of what worked and what did not. As I expanded my repertoire of knowledge, the workshop became my own.

Each year I ask students to purchase a journal, notebooks, and folders. Letters and forms for writers' workshop are distributed and explained. I then begin building our writing community. I begin community building in order to ease students into the school year. In addition, the activities involved in building a strong community help us know one another better and more fully—essentials for fostering writing (see Appendix 10). During my first year of using writers' workshop, I did not spend much time in this area, but I came to understand the importance of a strong community of writers as an incident occurred.

My mother had died two years earlier. In order to work through the grief, I wrote about her in my journal. I shared these writings with my students and read excerpts showing how many entries included thoughts of my mother. The students followed my lead and spent quiet time rehearsing and sorting through ideas found in their journals. When it was time for group share, Roger raised his hand. He began by saying, "I don't know if I can do this, but . . ." He then began reading an entry about his mother. He stopped reading and began crying uncontrollably. His mother, too, had died six years earlier. As I listened and tried to console him, my initial concern was the reactions of others in the class. My knowledge of adolescents and the cruelty they can project caused my fear. This was not only a student crying in the middle of class—this was a boy crying. I looked around at the faces of my students, but they weren't laughing. They were concerned for him. I could have hugged every single one of those students that day. They had come to accept and appreciate what each person had to say. The most important lesson that day for me was the importance of building a trusting community within a classroom of writers—a classroom that cares enough about what they say to share it, a community that respects enough to accept it.

Community building sets the tone for the year. It establishes expectations that we have for each other and the respect we each deserve when living and working together in a class. Community building must be done on a continual basis throughout the year in order to maintain a trusting and open environment in the classroom. Regrouping and reevaluating is a necessity in order to maintain an effective environment.

## Writing Begins

As we continue to build a trusting environment, we begin to write. I carefully explain each stage of the writing process. These stages later become part of a bulletin board that serves as reference for the first six weeks. We then begin rehearsal. As I demonstrate with my own journal, I explain to the students how to collect ideas for writing. I want students to understand, like I have come to understand, that writing is an extension of ourselves. I want them to see potential stories, poems, and essays in everything around them and in everything they do. Therefore, I read entries about my mother, show them cartoons I have collected, and share observations and pieces of my life. I describe the process I am taking with my own writing. I explain how writing develops over time as we think, share, and experiment. My students are encouraged to do the same as we embark on a new venture toward becoming writers through writers' workshop.

# The "Kinks" I Encountered

I have encountered many obstacles in my two short years of utilizing writers' workshop. I have discovered varying personalities and teaching styles must be considered when beginning a program of this nature. It is through experimentation with writers' workshop in your own classroom that you will find whether the "shoe fits." Atwell's shoes were much too large for me at the beginning. I had to find my own size and true fit. In order to find my way, I had to take other roads, try different methods and strategies that would ensure a good fit for me. It is through these obstacles I have learned to provide an environment in which my students and I will gain the most benefits.

### Can I Get Everything Done?

The first obstacle I faced was in the organization of the workshop. As I followed Atwell's (1987) ideas of teaching mini-lessons, conferencing with the students, providing time to write, having group share each day, and writing myself; I found it impossible to do it all. It was overwhelming. How did Atwell do all these things?

I knew students needed large amounts of quiet, uninterrupted time to write, and I tried hard to adhere to a specific schedule for writing, a time students could count on every day. But this was difficult. On some days my mini-lessons ran too long. On other days, if everyone had a particularly good day in writing, the group share time would run too long. From the onset, I incorporated readers' workshop as well as writers' workshop into my block. On the days new novels were introduced, students did not want to spend time writing; they wanted to immediately begin their books. Then again, on some days writing would cut into our reading time. To solve this problem, I tried doing readers' workshop two days a week and writers' workshop three days. The next week we would reverse the workshops. This also caused problems. If too many days were skipped, students had a difficult time getting into their writing. They would lose track of thoughts and become frustrated.

In addition to maintaining a consistent schedule for writing and instruction, I also faced a time constraint for both peer and teacher conferences. Teacher–student conferences were a necessity for me because I based my mini-lessons on the needs I noted within students' writing. Spending time with each student gave me insight into the strengths and weaknesses of individual student writers. It provided me with an individual annotated assessment of their progress. Students also needed time to conference with their peers. It was important for students to talk with their peers in order to gain insight and understanding different from that which I could provide. The problems were to find time to conference with every student, to allow students to conference with one another, to give extended periods of time to write, and to provide instruction. They seemed insurmountable until I took a realistic look at what I was doing.

I first looked at my method of instruction. I realized there were times when my reading and writing mini-lessons were similar, yet I spent fifteen minutes separately on each. I decided to combine my mini-lessons for both reading and writing. I used my novels to teach not only concepts of reading but also to introduce various styles and techniques of writing. For example, I might teach a lesson concerned with the development of plot in a short story. I discussed plot in a short story children were reading and then related how the development of plot works in writing. My students were able to see how writing and reading are interconnected—how one develops as the result of the other. The longer I combined my reading and writing mini-lessons, the more I was unable to discuss one without the other. They have become interchangeable in my mind and in the minds of my students. They are benefiting from the integration because they see and understand the connection between reading and writing. My one mini-lesson now takes approximately twenty minutes, which opens up fifteen to twenty minutes each day for more student writing time.

Once I had a handle on mini-lessons and writing, I tackled the problem of conferencing. Teacher-student conferences were the most difficult; finding time to meet with every student each week and maintaining order among the other students was a challenge. I eventually developed a schedule whereby I met with five students per day. Students were assigned a day each week to meet with me to discuss areas of need. In this way, I could conference individually with each student at least once a week. These conferences were held at my desk away from the quiet writing group. Peer conferences were held in isolated corners of the room, again, away from the quiet writing areas.

As I struggled to find my own way in writers' workshop, I came to realize that I had to develop schedules and time lines that met my style of teaching and the personalities of my students. Three components became the basis for each writers' workshop: I would provide as much time as possible for student writing, provide lessons on the skills and crafts necessary to become more effective writers and readers, and provide a scheduled time for conferences with me and with each other. I learned to listen to my students. They became my best source for knowing when to instruct and conference and when to let them go.

## What Is Rehearsal?

Once I solved some of the basic mechanical "kinks" of the workshop, I was faced with my most challenging obstacle. How do I promote and encourage writing? Rehearsal, in particular, gave me the most difficulty. In the two years I have been using writers' workshop, the inevitable statement always arises: "I don't have anything to write about." I have come to expect this statement as I expect the sun to rise and set every day. The voice at the beginning of the year is truly asking for a jump start to writing. Sometimes these students are spurred on by a few questions such as, "Did you see or observe anything interesting or out of the ordinary today?" "Is there something you keep thinking about today?" "Did anything happen at home this morning while you were getting ready for school?" Usually students receive a spark before too many questions have been asked. There are times, however, when questions do not work and no topics are forthcoming. I have come to realize over the past two years, however, that topic selection is not all there is to rehearsal.

When I began writers' workshop, I did not fully understand the concept of rehearsal and, therefore, did not spend as much time on it as I should have. My goal in rehearsal was to encourage students to view their journals as a place where future writing is born. Yet I continued to hear diary entries about friends, family, pets, and occurrences at school. Students then took one of these entries, rewrote it, and turned it in. I realized they were using these entries as first drafts. The journals were a storage place for future ideas to use as topics for writing. The journals were not places for completed pieces to be born. The students saw these journal entries as drafts and, worse, as final pieces. I realized more time and guidance needed to occur in the area of rehearsal.

Much of my students' lack of rehearsal stemmed from my lack of understanding. When I began writers' workshop, I viewed rehearsal as a place to find topics for writing. As I grew in knowledge, I began to think about the term "rehearsal" as more than simply practicing, brainstorming ideas, or prewriting. I began to view it as the part of the process that encourages writers to pull emotions and experiences from the past, present, and future. Using the analogy of an actor in a play, it is more than simply reading the lines in a script; it is the experiences, actions, feelings, and emotions which the actor brings to a character before the actual act of practicing or rehearsal can begin. Like the actor, the writer only begins rehearsal after much reflection based upon experiences in his or her life.

When I was first began to write, the time I spent rehearsing was considerably shorter than it was for my students. I could gather my thoughts, organize ideas, formulate a plan of action, choose a genre from which to write, and consider an audience much more quickly. I, after all, had lived longer and had more experiences in my lifetime, and therefore, my repertoire of ideas was much more abundant. What I failed to consider with my students was their inexperience with life and the observations they had not achieved in their eleven to thirteen years of living. They needed more time to "live" with rehearsal before they began writing. They needed practice in how to look again or revisit the world around them, but differently somehow, as through an artist's eyes—a writer's eyes.

I began to experiment with ideas and activities to enhance my students' observation skills and bring to light past experiences that could be revisited in their minds. One activity students loved, and we all had fun with, was observing an ordinary potato. Students were given their own potato. They were to observe it closely by looking at it from every angle, touching it, smelling it, and examining it microscopically through their own eyes for every detail. It was their potato and they had to spend time getting to know it. They wrote about their potato descriptively, with some even giving it human qualities. The potatoes were then spread on a table, at which time students had to find their own. This served as a simple, fun exercise to demonstrate to students the importance of observation skills and how writing can occur through ordinary observances. Students were taught how to observe the seemingly unimportant details that might serve as impetus for writing. They learned to look at the simple, but saw the potential for writing about it extraordinarily.

Another activity that served the purpose of reflecting on past experiences was a lesson designed around developing a character. Together we made up a fictional character, and decided on a gender and a name. For example, we might give our character the male gender and call him Bob. I then asked the students, "How old is Bob?" In my experience, most students want him to be an age anywhere from thirty to eighty, so I would reply, "What do you really know about a person that age?" At this time, I stressed the importance of writing about what they know. Since they are between the ages of eleven and thirteen, they have more experiences with understanding this age group and could, therefore, write more effectively. I continued with questions like, "What does Bob look like?" "How does he feel?" "What does Bob love?" "What does Bob hate?" "What do other people think about Bob?" While doing this exercise, the questions lead students to develop a character with specific physical, emotional, and social qualities. These qualities are based on the students' knowledge of themselves and others around them. In order to develop Bob, they have to reflect and pull from events in their past. It serves as a way to encourage and promote self-reflection and prior knowledge—two essentials necessary to engage in effective rehearsal.

I now realize rehearsal is the most important stage in the writing process. It is a place for beginnings; a place for seeds of thought to be planted, watered, and nourished; a place to write ideas, observations, words overheard, and dreams dreamed. Rehearsal is like throwing various packets of flower seeds into an uncultivated garden. You aren't quite sure which flowers will erupt from that untilled soil, or which ones will continue to grow and flourish. You know, however, if you throw enough seeds a few will grow to become beautiful flowers to be cared for and nourished. Your garden becomes a place of beauty. Young writers, in like manner, are a garden where seeds of thought are planted, nourished, and encouraged to grow. Rehearsal is the place where thoughts and ideas are tilled, watered, and fed. It is from rehearsal that beautiful pieces of writing emerge.

Based on my readings and discussions with colleagues, I now have a new direction for rehearsal. I plan to increase the amount of time I spend on it, possibly an entire six weeks. I want students to have a huge bank account of ideas for writing—one they can add to and draw from throughout the year. Ideas for starting this account may include the following:

Collect names to use as characters.
Collect settings to use based on places students have seen or visited.
Collect words and interesting vocabulary.
Create conflicts and problems that can occur in the plots of their stories.
Collect various themes.
Work on interesting leads and titles.
Keep a list of strong, vivid verbs, metaphors, similes, and personifications.
Collect dreams and goals.
Write conversations between characters.
Observe and collect characteristics of people, both physical and emotional.

This list is only a beginning, but it is one that will enable me to encourage children to look at the world around them in order to make a story grow.

## Listen Closely and You Will Hear . . .

As the school year progresses, writing takes on a life of its own. Stories are written, poems are shared, and new insights are uncovered. Yet, I begin to hear a new voice. It is a demanding voice and one that permeates throughout the class. "Writing is boring!" "I hate this class!" "All we ever do is write!" I know during the year students' repertoires of writing ideas become depleted and they become frustrated. More than anything, however, they need someone or something to blame. I become that scapegoat. I have had some students, during these outbursts, become disrespectful and rebellious against the whole writing process. At this point I have suggested to students that they write about their frustrations. Stephanie was one of those students who rebelled and wrote about it. As Stephanie's anger poured out on paper about me and the writing process, a surprising event occurred. She was no longer "stuck" on having anything to write about. This anger served as an impetus for her to continue writing. It caused her to physically engage in the act of writing, which helped to revive the "flow of her creative juices."

*Stephanie takes out her frustrations through writing and finds she has something to say.*

> They are disrespectfull and hatefull.
> This story is going nowhere. I can't
> write. If my life depending on writting
> a story every week I'd already be
> dead. I hate writing. It just ain't
> my thing. The reason why I can't write
> is because of my stubborness. I said
> I ain't going to like writing so it's
> in my mind. I don't. So I won't.
>
> Stephanie Davis

Because other students were displaying similar frustrations over the whole writing process, I asked them to literally illustrate the process by drawing it. Elissa's interpretation of the writing process depicted a seed growing to maturity.

*Elissa demonstrates her view of the writing process through her drawing.*

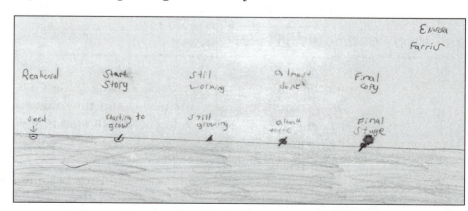

Greg sees himself enclosed within a box, all alone with no distractions; alone with only his ideas.

*Greg finds peace through writing.*

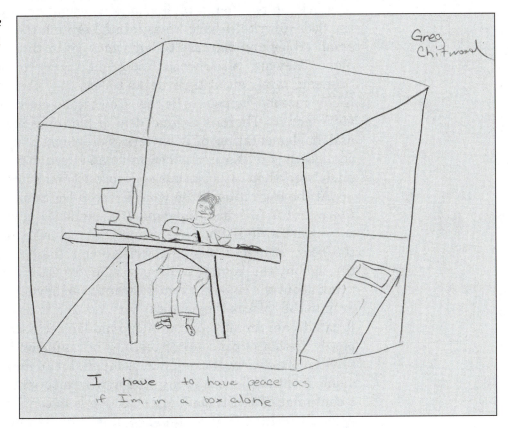

Through these drawings, I was able to determine where frustrations existed and where they did not. Although frustrations were evident, students did indeed know and understand the writing process. I realized, however, the process was not the same for everyone. I also discovered something about myself and my role in the writers' workshop. Only a very few students drew me as part of the process. Most students did not. I was an absent participant. While some students needed someone to blame for their frustrations, the majority saw me as an outsider to the process. I discovered my role as a teacher is to look beyond what I see and understand what a writer may be telling me.

## Visit the Writers' Workshop—You Might Decide to Stay

The entire structure of the classroom changes with a workshop format. There is more movement and more discussions between and among students. Students are not on the same page at the same time. Some may be writing while others may be conferencing. Some students may be using reference books scattered about the room while some may be using the computer. The arrangement of the room changes as well. In addition to providing two comfortable chairs, I also allow my students to sit on the floor to write. I have areas located around the room equipped with small tables and chairs. Students may go to these areas to be totally alone. They may also choose to seek out a quiet corner of the classroom. Students rarely sit at their desks unless they choose to do so. What at first glance may appear to be chaos, on second glance is a well-structured environment. There is a great deal of planning involved in the design and implementation of a writers' workshop. The role of the teacher changes only in the area of becoming an effective manager. This is, after all, a "workshop." It looks busy because students are busy doing work.

At the beginning of the year, I read a Dr. Seuss book called *Oh, the Places You'll Go!* (see Appendix 15). Students new to a middle school setting are afraid—they are unsure as to what to expect. Upon reading the book, students talk and write about the "places" they might go throughout the year. We discuss their expectations for the year and think about the goals they might want to achieve. Writing can take children to the "places they want to go." Writing is powerful. It can soothe. It can dream dreams. It can uncap hidden recesses of the mind. It can piece together our disjointed feelings of confusion and help us see ourselves more clearly. It can make us laugh. It can make us feel we are not alone. As Michelle, one of my students, so eloquently put it, "Writing is a continuation of the soul. My objective is to continue 'paused writing.' After all, writing is never finished, it is only paused in time."

# CHAPTER 8

## Changes

## Virginia Wadleigh

*Sometimes something beautiful can happen in the midst of a maelstrom. I teach eighth grade in a middle school, and the best class writing I have encountered resulted from a tragedy. It began with the unfortunate horror of two middle school students shooting, killing, and wounding adults and children alike. What began as a buzz the day following the incident escalated as students talked more and more about the shooting.*

*On day three after the shootings, the students were still talking. I decided this was a "teachable moment" and maybe by talking and writing about the killings and injuries, my students would be better able to process the horror. My prepared lesson plans went out the window as I gave an overview of what had happened at the middle school. I asked each student to add something they had heard or read about the shootings or tell the class how they felt. I was awestruck by the responses I got. If you teach this age group, you know there is at least one student who must "walk on" or disturb another person's discourse. This did not happen. For all three of my classes, there was complete silence and respectful listening while the discussions took place. The thoughts of the students varied from: "They should be given life imprisonment" to "They're sick!"*

*At this point, I asked my students to write about the situation. They could select any literary genre to write in and choose any point of view. I simply wanted them to write. In previous workshop sessions, some students had started writing immediately while others took longer to begin. That day, there was no hesitation. They all had something to say, and the total quality of their writing was high. I was amazed at the depth and breadth of what they wrote. It was at this moment I knew that my life, as a teacher of the writer, would change.*

*Abby writes her feelings about the shooting.*

## Pain

Why the children did it nobody knows

The answer lies deep in their souls

Some parents feel very alone

Because one decides to take their own

They have to come to terms with their deaths

But in some hearts, it will never rest

The boys should realize

That they took some lives

But the punishment probably won't suit

The children will deny the truth.

Abby Palmer

In the beginning it was our language arts department chairperson who said, "We need to think about making the most of our language arts block. We need to examine the idea of integrating our writing, reading, and English." I had always taught these subjects separately, teaching reading through the use of short stories, novels, and poetry, and English skills through formal lessons. Integrating the subjects was an interesting idea.

As I read, discussed, listened, and reflected on the concept of integration I began the airplane ride of my career. I took off slowly because I wasn't at all sure the pilot had the right fuel mixture to get the plane off the ground. At times the flight has been smooth sailing, but more often than not, it has been a bumpy trip. As a beginner in the workshop approach, I was introduced to Atwell's (1987) *In the Middle*. By using this text, various inservices, colleagues' brains, flexible students, and a supportive principal, I have helped my students make vast improvements as readers and writers. I have become a better teacher because I was forced to examine the craft of reading and writing from the ground up.

The purpose of this chapter is to share my experiences, both failures and successes. In order to accomplish this, I need to describe the planning that went into the first "flight" and how I let go of previous methodology. I will introduce you to the first six weeks I taught writers' workshop. In addition, I will share reflections from the end of that first year and the new horizons I see ahead.

## The Workshop

At the beginning of my first year of incorporating the workshop technique, I implemented readers' workshop. I had been introduced to both readers' and writers' workshops the week before the beginning of school. I knew I did not have enough prior planning time to integrate both, therefore, I reasoned, if I took six weeks to get readers' workshop off the ground, then the following six weeks I could pull in writers' workshop. It was easier for me to initially implement readers' workshop because I had a vast array of fiction books written by contemporary young adult authors. I was already teaching the "skills" of reading using novels, short stories, and poetry, so I felt it would take less time to organize readers' workshop, and to a certain extent that concept worked.

Both workshops are designed to build better readers and writers by giving students time to read and write. I, therefore, began readers' workshop by allocating a large chunk of time for students to read. I gave them choices as to the books they read, and ownership was encouraged through the choices students made. I felt by beginning readers' workshop with choice, time, and ownership, it would make for an easier transition into writers' workshop for my students and me.

# The Beginning

I began my workshop with dialogue notebooks (Atwell, 1987). While students used these notebooks to respond to their reading, writing responses to books laid the groundwork for future writing. We also began a writer's log, which later provided "starters" for student writing. Folders were distributed, and each day I asked students to write about something they had seen or something that had happened to them. In this way, students began to observe their surroundings; they became cognizant of the happenings within their lives. I set up "permanent" hanging folders in a box for their writing logs and future works in progress.

As a class we talked about the things students were writing in their logs—the ideas that would later become stories to share. We discussed where their entries came from and what situations occurred that sparked ideas. In addition, we brainstormed ways that published authors obtain ideas for writing. We listed things such as real-life incidents, dreams, future plans, and feelings. I also used children's literature as a discussion tool. Books such as *Be Good to Eddie Lee* by Virginia Fleming, *The Paper Bag Princess* by Robert Munsch, and *Mama Don't Allow* by Tacher Hurd were chosen because of their rich subject matter and the everyday experiences to which my students could relate (see Appendix 15). We discussed the possible origins of these authors' ideas. The students hypothesized that perhaps Fleming had a relative or a friend with Down syndrome. Maybe, as a child, Robert Munsch was made fun of because he had shabby clothes to wear and through writing, he was able to deal with the hurt. Perhaps Tacher Hurd's brother played a trumpet and the author couldn't stand the noise. The reasons were varied and numerous. This exercise gave my students an understanding of topics and authors' choices. Many times writers find their ideas from everyday occurrences. My students soon began to appreciate their lives and the stories they had to tell.

As a group, we decided to spend five to eight minutes every other day jotting down ideas: things students saw, questions they had, or thoughts that occurred to them. They were building a log of ideas—ideas they could turn to when they began to write. In the beginning students struggled with their writing logs. As the weeks passed, however, I found the students no longer hesitated when writing in their logs. They were able to write ideas quickly and efficiently. There was less "wait time" and, for the most part, students retrieved their logs as they entered the room. While I had yet to begin the full-blown writers' workshop, I considered these logs part of the preparation.

While readers' workshop was relatively easy to implement, writers' workshop was more of a challenge. As a teacher of English, I had always taught writing in a structured, formal way. I included a section on creative writing, and I sometimes allowed free choice in topic selection.

Primarily, however, I was the "teacher type" who presented a prompt, setting, cartoon, or picture to help students begin the writing process. I failed to recognize how this might take away ownership from children's writing until I began reading and studying about the technique. In Nancie Atwell's words, "Writers in a workshop can exert ownership because they're not waiting for the teacher's motivational pre-writing activity or directions for 'fixing' a piece of writing; instead, they're using the tools and procedures at their disposal to motivate and improve their own writing. Their writing belongs to them and they are responsible for it" (1987, p. 64). I wanted to hit myself in the head. It made all the sense in the world! I had understood choice and ownership in readers' workshop but had failed to see the similarity in writers' workshop. If I provided the prompt, it was not the students' own writing. They did not own it. I was determined to make a change from the teacher control method to the workshop method, and change I did! I changed my teaching style from a structured format with daily lessons and practice into a flowing overlap of the three disciplines of English, reading, and spelling. Because of block scheduling, I was given more sustained time to demonstrate the connections between reading and writing.

Although my teaching style was in a state of change there were certain restrictions placed on me and parameters I had to consider as I began writers' workshop. I teach between seventy-five and eighty students per day. This requires a great deal of planning and organization in order to meet the individual needs of all students as the workshop technique purports to do. In addition, there are required skills set forth by the county curriculum guide that must be taught and tested. Students are required to take a standardized test and show measurable progress in each of the core areas in order to prove that I am doing my job as a teacher. My state also requires that each student write a timed, twenty-minute, three point essay on a predetermined prompt. These parameters became the challenges I had to overcome. I had to determine how to move these established parameters, including state- and county-mandated grammar skills, into writers' workshop and still allow the students to have ownership of their writing. It wasn't easy, but within these parameters, I began my version of writers' workshop.

## Writers' Workshop

As the end of the first six weeks drew closer, I became more apprehensive about beginning writers' workshop. I asked myself over and over, "Am I able to do justice to writers' workshop?" Luckily, I was able to receive support from inservices and question-and-answer sessions, and, perhaps most importantly, encouragement from colleagues. No matter how much or how little I was able to accomplish, I was encouraged to move forward. Little by little I began to jump into writers' workshop. I reread Atwell's (1987) book and began to focus on the aspects I felt I could use in my environment.

### Getting Ready

One of the first things I noticed in Atwell's writers' workshop was the enormous source of supplies she maintained (Atwell, 1987, p.63). I did not have a source for writing supplies, so that portion of the workshop was out for me. I did manage to get two folders for every student. I established my conference centers, and it was time to start!

Each step I took was preceded by Atwell's suggestions. I read and reread her book in order to move myself forward in the workshop. I began by explaining to my students that I would be using a new teaching method that would turn them into better writers. I wanted the students to know, up front, the process would be as new to me as it was to them and if some aspect of the workshop did not work, we would try something else. I felt I had to be truthful with my students. Eighth graders have a wonderful capacity for knowing when you are being less than honest. Therefore, I told them the technique had proven effective with other eighth graders and we would do our best to make it work for us. I gave an overview of writers' workshop and discussed the four routines as well as the rules (see Tables 8.1 and 8.2). My students copied the rules for writers' workshop in their logs as well as verbalized them. I wanted to make certain they understood each rule and routine, as this would be our guide throughout the remainder of the year.

**TABLE 8.1   Rules for Writers' Workshop**

1. Write on one side of the paper only.
2. No erasing.
3. Save everything, even the smallest scrap of paper.
4. Date and label everything.
5. Speak in quiet voices only.
6. Check with the teacher before going to conference centers.

**TABLE 8.2   Routines of Writers' Workshop**

| | |
|---|---|
| 1–2 minutes | "Status of Class" report (Atwell, 1987) |
| 5–10 minutes | Skills mini-lesson |
| 20–30 minutes | Actual writing time |
| 10 minutes | Group share |

Procedural issues were discussed next. I revised many of Atwell's (1987) suggestions in order to make them my own. Procedures needed to meet the needs of my students. Therefore, I identified several components for which I felt students should be responsible (see Table 8.3). Each item was explained and discussed to the extent that it became routine. The procedures we established at the beginning would maintain us throughout the year.

**TABLE 8.3** **Student's Role**

1. When you come to class, you are responsible for getting your writing folder from the file.
2. Next, plan what you will do today in your writing.
3. Begin working.
4. Care about the things you write.
5. Don't be afraid to try different ways or types of writing.
6. Remember to date each piece and use revision numbers (as needed) for each writing piece.
7. When you edit your final draft, use a pencil/pen that is different in color from the paper you are working on.
8. Check the posted skills list and unit spelling words to verify inclusion.
9. Recognize what is successful in your writing and how you can improve on what's not successful.
10. Please make certain that you don't do anything that distracts or disturbs other students or me.
11. Discover what writing can do for you.

### The Writing Begins

Once the rules and procedures had been set, we began to write. The groundwork had been laid for topic selection through the writing logs already begun. In order to continue the students' "ideas" list, I discussed memories as a way to further develop topics for writing. I slowly and deliberately read a passage from Atwell (1987): "Now would you sit quietly and think, as I thought this morning, about the stories you have to tell? Remember when you were a child. Remember laughing and crying. Remember frights and quarrels and loving people. Remember moments in life that you want to preserve" (p. 80).

I read it twice as students' heads lay on their desks and then I let them remember. After a short time, I asked them to pick up their pencils and begin writing a memory. About 90 percent of the class began to write. Some of them didn't want to stop; they had become involved in their writing just as they had when asked to write about the murdered middle school students. It was exciting! What wasn't exciting, however, was the 10 percent who had blank papers. I reread the passage and two more students slowly began to write. There was a third student who could not grasp a memory. I stretched, pulled, prodded, and finally suggested he sketch a memory and then transfer that sketch into words. My persistence finally paid off and the student began writing. The students were given twenty more minutes to write. I then placed them in small groups where they shared the memories they had written. I was somewhat surprised when some students did not want to share. At the time I did not want to pressure anyone, so I let it go. In retrospect, I should have insisted on everyone saying a few words. It wasn't a tragic error, and the good news was I had made it through the first day of writers' workshop.

We continued writers' workshop three days a week for the rest of that six-week period. The other two days were spent engaged in readers' workshop. The students soon learned the flow of the workshop. Each day we began with the "status of the class" (Atwell, 1987, p. 91). This is a time when students identify where they are in the process. It requires that students become knowledgeable about the stages of the writing process and learn to be able to recognize where they are in that process. This was a must for me in that it gave me insight into how students were progressing through their writing. Next, a mini-lesson was conducted where a skill or literary craft was presented. Writing followed. During writing time, my goal was to conference with each student every day and end the session with group share. While it all sounded relatively easy on paper, the reality was quite different.

## Crossroads and Baggage

I tried to follow Atwell's (1987) format, but I soon found out I could not do it all. I became frustrated and blamed myself and my inability to conduct the workshop. I felt I was unorganized and inept. What had begun as a pleasurable plane ride had suddenly become quite bumpy. As I embarked upon the ride, I encountered many potholes along the runway—potholes that Atwell seemed to handle quite well, but I could not seem to master. I brought old traditions and excess baggage into this endeavor and I was finding out quickly what stumbling blocks they were.

## Instruction

I had been trained to teach in a traditional manner. I introduced a lesson, explained the concept, modeled, used guided practice, had students engage in independent practice, and used formal applications. As I dove into writers' workshop, however, I realized my traditional "upbringing" would no longer work. I could see the benefits of writers' workshop. I had witnessed the power by which writing could move students. But I could not determine how to "teach" that power. I felt my students would be better writers if allowed to write, if only I could untangle the secret of instruction.

Based on all my readings and the in-services in which I had participated, I became aware of the fact that children learn best through the application of skills rather than through isolated practice and rote memorization. *What? Let go of guided and independent practice? How would students ever learn the rules of grammar unless they practiced? How could they learn if all they did was write?* Even though my traditions were screaming in my head, one of the first changes I made was to eliminate grammar skill practice.

I listened to the authorities and began teaching mini-lessons each day at the beginning of writers' workshop. The topics of the lessons were based on several factors. I do not follow the English textbook in a sequential order—I never have. I do, however, follow the curriculum guide for my county. In this guide, topics that must be covered during a year are listed. Again, there is no specific order I follow. I try to base my lessons on what my students need in their writing. This is not always possible because of the wide-ranging ability levels within an eighth grade class. Based on many years of experience, I have a good idea of the skills my students need. Therefore, the topics I select for mini-lessons come from that knowledge.

Once I had taught a skill in a mini-lesson, students were free to write. The skill would be placed on the skills list, and I encouraged them to use the new skill in their writing as much as possible. As I observed and conferenced with individual students, questions were asked concerning the skills covered. I made notes as to which students had acquired the skill and which students continued to need help. There were times when I could tell that very few students fully understood a particular skill. At that time, I reverted back to my traditional worksheets and practice exercises.

What I found throughout this first year was that most students learned their skills by using them in their writing. The authorities had been right. Although I struggled with letting drill and practice go completely, I discovered that students do, indeed, acquire the necessary skills through their writing. It worked!

### Spelling

A second bit of baggage that I brought along with me as I began writers' workshop was the issue of spelling. Traditionally, the language arts grade on the report card was divided into three areas: reading, spelling, and English. According to the county guidelines, spelling as a subject counted as a separate grade. Contrary to this notion, however, is the belief that spelling should not be taught as an isolated subject (Laminack & Wood, 1996; Wilde, 1990). To memorize and spell a list of words does not necessarily transfer into better reading or writing. It was suggested that I try to incorporate spelling into writing. I could teach short spelling lessons on patterns, form, and strategies during mini-lessons and then show their relationship to writing. I was strongly urged not to isolate spelling from writing.

This was totally new to me. I had always taught spelling in the traditional format, where students are given a list of words each week, engage in practice exercises, and take a test on Friday. I also had a spelling book to follow, with thirty-six separate spelling lists and lessons that had to be taught. I could not see a way to integrate all thirty-six lessons into several short mini-lessons. To add to this dilemma, teachers in my state are assessed by the increase in individual student knowledge from one year to the next. Counties are compared with each other, and schools are also compared to other schools for improvement in achievement scores. I was responsible for seeing that my students were learning age-appropriate words and meanings.

I believed students needed to learn new words in order to increase their vocabulary, and I did not fully believe they could do this if spelling was incorporated into writing with no direct instruction and memorization. I knew I could change to mini-lessons and incorporate some spelling in student writing. The one thing I could not change was having my students learn twenty new words each week. This is a tradition I have not been able to break. I do make some attempts to incorporate spelling into writing by asking my students to use their spelling words in their writing pieces. We keep a list of words studied, and students must use a minimum number of spelling words in each new piece of writing.

While some of my traditional baggage was discarded, some was not. I discovered that I had to take the suggestions of authorities and assimilate them into my belief system. As I continue to learn more about writing, perhaps more traditions can be discarded. For now, however, I have to do what feels right for me.

# Things That Go Bump in the Night

As I reflect on the first six-week session of writers' workshop, the difficulties stand out more than the successes. There were two areas with which I was frustrated: conducting and maintaining conferences and evaluating student writing.

## *Conferences*

Conferencing presented the first problem. I established three conference areas in corners of my room. Each corner had a small table and two chairs where students talked to one another about their writing. At the same time pairs of students were conferencing, I was conducting teacher–student conferences. The problem quickly arose with the corner conference areas. Students began to take advantage of the situation. Because I was busy discussing the writing of their classmates, conference partners became distracted from their task. They began discussing everything from hairstyles to who did what to whom last night. I also noticed some students were getting other students to do their work during these conferences. I was at a loss. I had read about conferences, but could not visualize how to handle them. Modeling would have had helped, but I had done none and I felt uncomfortable demonstrating something I had never seen. It wasn't until I developed a checklist system of my own that conference centers became learning environments for my students and me.

As I began the second six-week session of writers' workshop, I made two important changes. The first change I made was the way in which students went to the conference areas. Previously, anyone who needed help went to a conference area and stayed as long as necessary. I began the new six weeks with a sign-up sheet. Each person who needed a conference had to sign up. The first two pairs conferenced together for five minutes. At the end of the five minutes they returned to their desks and the next two students entered into a conference. This worked well. We now had a system and students were adhering to it.

The second change concerned the conference itself. I needed some way to ensure that students remained on task during student-to-student conference time. I used a checklist that each student was asked to complete before and after the conference (see Appendix 9). This checklist forced students to identify an area of need in their writing before the conference took place. It also ensured that talk would focus on writing throughout the conference.

The organization and management of conferences had been the difficult part. Once I developed and implemented the sign-up sheets and the checklists, I felt I had conquered this particular challenge.

## Evaluation

Early in my readings and discussions with other teachers we talked about evaluation techniques. We discussed the definition of evaluation and the difference between it and assessment. We questioned and argued the sensibility of evaluation. We debated about how best to show progress, build self-esteem, *and* determine grades for report cards. Evaluation was no easy matter to handle.

After much conversation I decided how I would handle the issue of grades and determine criteria for those grades. I felt parents wanted to see a product that had been graded. Even though I was beginning to believe the process of writing was more important than the product, I knew parents related to the product. Therefore, each six weeks students selected one piece they had written and completed. A skills checklist (see Appendices 11, 12, 13, and 14) was provided whereby students could edit their writing for skills taught during mini-lessons throughout that grading period. For example, if one of the skills taught was the correct use of dialogue, then I wanted to see the correct use of dialogue in their writing. A skills sheet was attached to each student's writing, and as I evaluated the piece, I checked for correct skill usage.

A second way I assessed students was by the progress they had made from one six-week period to the next. I wanted to determine whether or not their writing technique was improving. Therefore, when students turned in their completed product for a given six weeks, they also had to turn in their previous graded writing. Before evaluating the current product, I scanned my comments from the previous writing, making note of the suggestions made and errors corrected. The current product would then be assessed with those things in mind. I felt students were growing in their writing ability if they had taken the suggestions made and incorporated them into their current product of writing.

My system of evaluation is not without its flaws, and I continue to struggle. Perhaps as I gain more experience with writers' workshop, someday I will find a better method. For now students are a part of the evaluation process by making their own choice of what is to be evaluated. This along with the skills sheet has worked for me.

# Up, Up, and Away

The second year of writers' workshop brought changes. I began with a group of eighth graders who, for the most part, had been exposed to writers' workshop the previous year. Ninety percent or more knew the steps in the writing process. One of the most important things I did was spend the first five days of school building a community in our class-room. At this age students are insecure. I wanted to make sure every-one knew each other so we could feel comfortable in making mistakes as well as sharing successes.

The first thing I did was create a bulletin board entitled "All About Me." On the board I included photographs, mementos, and artifacts of importance in my life. Items included photographs of my family and friends, book covers, and a picture of the earth to represent my travels. On the first day of class I discussed the items on my bulletin board. The students asked questions and at the end of our time I told them they would be doing the same thing with their own bulletin board. I placed a large yellow sheet of butcher paper on the wall and titled it "All About You." Students began bringing in their own mementos of family, friends, and hobbies. As each student talked about his or her mementos, class-mates asked questions and made comments. We were on our way to knowing one another better.

During that first week of community building, we began discussing ways to learn information about others through interviews. I read an interview written about the group Smashing Pumpkins, and we talked about what makes an effective interview. Students were randomly paired to begin the process. As each student was interviewed notes were taken. Students were then asked to write an "article" about their part-ner. The articles were shared with the entire class. In this way, we were able to learn more about one another.

Another day we spent determining what makes up a community. I began by using our own town as an example. We discussed the character-istics of our town and the things that must be present in order to maintain a smooth-running community. We then transferred the characteristics of our town to our own community in the classroom. We developed a list of necessary components by which we lived the remainder of the year.

In retrospect, these first five days made a tremendous impact on my students and served to set the tone for the entire year. Through commu-nity building my students felt safe in their environment. They were much more willing to share opinions, discuss writing, and show their vulnerability. Because everyone played a part in forming the commu-nity, my students felt a sense of belonging (see Appendix 10).

Although community building made a great impact on my students, perhaps the best thing that happened to me was during the summer before my second year. I attended a "Bill Martin Pathways to Literacy Conference." There I met some wonderful people and learned more about the writing process. I learned new techniques and ideas to make writers' workshop more effective for promoting student writing.

Not every idea I was introduced to became an immediate fixture in my class. One idea, however, proved to be especially enriching to my students. The idea involved sharing and publishing student writing. In November students contributed writing pieces for publication. The pieces were bound into two booklets, each containing ten to twelve writing pieces. I took the booklets to my local dentist, who placed them in his waiting room for people to read. It worked! Patients waiting for appointments read the stories and poems. They even laughed out loud at some of them. Other stories made them think! My students were proud of themselves. More importantly, they considered themselves authors.

Looking back at my experiences, the first words of wisdom I would give to a beginner are "be prepared!" I am glad I jumped into that first year with both feet, but it was too soon, too fast. I don't feel as if my first-year workshop students suffered, but they were the crew that helped the real workshop get off the ground during the second year. I learned to use writers' workshop in ways with which I feel most comfortable. I learned to follow my own instincts rather than adhere strictly to the suggestions of others. The past two years have been a great learning experience—years full of change. I know my students are better writers. I know I am a better teacher. I discovered it is only through change that we grow.

## Farewell

*Katie writes of change as she bids farewell to eighth grade.*

It's now time to leave behind
Two years at a school that we have survived
There are so many memories good and bad.
And all these we carry with us in our lives.

In all of this confusion,
We feel so many mixed feelings and thoughts.
We feel pain, love, relief, and regret.
So many things we could've done, so many things
now gone and lost.

There comes a time to make a choice about friendship
Which to keep in our hearts and which outcries to mend.
Whether to forgive lost friends, forget painful words said,
Whether to keep new friendships going on
or bring them to an end.

We all face new challenges,
We have new hopes, dreams, and fears.
While some leave with a smile on their face,
Others leave with eyes full of tears.

It's so hard to belive we're now "highschoolers,"
That we've made it this far.
Everyone going their own way, some left behind,
Others moving away out of reach, so far.

It's time to say good-bye, so long, seyonara,
For some it's the end, others a new beginning.
We don't know what will happen, or what to make of it
We can only sit and wait, and see what the future
brings!

By Katie Onks

# References

Applebee, A. (1984). *Contexts for learning to write: Studies of secondary school instruction*. Norwood, NJ: Ablex.

Atwell, N. (1987). *In the middle: Writing, reading, and learning with adolescents*. Portsmouth, NH: Heinemann.

Bereiter, C. (1980). Development in writing. In L. Gregg & E. Steinberg (Eds.), *Cognitive process in writing* (pp. 73–93). Hillsdale, NJ: Erlbaum.

Bergeron, B. (1990). What does the term whole language mean? Constructing a definition from literature. *Journal of Reading Behavior, 22*, 301–329.

Bomer, R. (1995). *Time for meaning*. Portsmouth, NH: Heinemann.

Calkins, L. (1983). *Lessons from a child*. Portsmouth, NH: Heinemann.

Calkins, L. (1986). *The art of teaching writing* (1st ed.). Portsmouth, NH: Heinemann.

Calkins, L. (1994). *The art of teaching writing* (2nd ed.). Portsmouth, NH: Heinemann.

Elbow, P. (1973). *Writing without teachers*. New York: Oxford University Press.

Elkind, D. (1989). *Miseduation*. New York: Knopf.

Emig, J. (1971). *The composing process of twelfth graders*. Urbana, IL: National Council of Teachers of English.

Flower, L., & Hayes, J. (1981). A cognitive process theory of writing. *College Composition and Communication, 32*, 365–387.

Funk, G. D., & Funk, H. D. (1989). Roadblocks to implementing the writing process. *The Clearing House, 62*, 222–224.

Goodman, Y. (1978). Kidwatching: An alternative to testing. *The National Elementary Principal*, *57*(4), 41–45.

Graves, D. H. (1975). An examination of the writing processes of seven-year-old children. *Research in the Teaching of English*, *9*, 227–241.

Graves, D. H. (1983). *Writing: Teachers and children at work*. Portsmouth, NH: Heinemann.

Graves, D. H. (1994). *A fresh look at writing*. Portsmouth, NH: Heinemann.

Harste, J., Woodward, V., & Burke, C. (1984). Examining our assumptions: A transactional view of literacy and learning. *Research in the Teaching of English*, *18*, 84–108.

Laminack, L., & Wood, K. (1996). *Spelling in use*. Urbana, IL: National Council of Teachers of English.

Moffett, J. (1983). *Teaching the universe of discourse*. Portsmouth, NH: Heinemann.

Montessori, M. (1912). *The Montessori method: Scientific pedagogy as applied to child education in the "Children's Houses" with additions and revisions by the author*. (A. E. George, Trans.) New York: Frederick A. Stokes.

Murray, D. M. (1978). Internal revision: A process of discovery. In C. R. Cooper & L. Odell (Eds.), *Research on composing: Points of departure* (pp. 85–103). Urbana, IL: National Council of Teachers of English.

Perl, S. (1983). How teachers teach the writing process. *The Elementary School Journal*, *84*(1), 20–24.

Piaget, J. (1969). *The language and thought of the child*. New York: World.

Rousseau, J. J. (1964). *Emile*. New York: Dutton.

Scardamalia, M. (1982). How children cope with the cognitive demands of writing. In C. H. Frederiksen, M. S. Whiteman, & J. F. Dominic (Eds.), *Writing: The nature, development, and teaching of written communication* (pp. 81–103). Hillsdale, NJ: Erlbaum.

Shanklin, N. L. (1991). Whole language and the writing process: One movement or two? *Topics in Language Disorder*, *11*(3), 45–57.

Smith, F. (1988). *Joining the Literacy Club*. Portsmouth, NH: Heinemann.

Stanek, L. (1994). *Thinking like a writer*. New York: Random House.

Wilde, S. (1990). A proposal for a new spelling curriculum. *Elementary School Journal*, *90*(3), 275–289.

# APPENDIX 1

# Sample Letter to Parents Concerning Spelling

Dear Parents,

I am so glad to have your child in my class this year. We will be embarking on a journey that will take your child to places he/she only dreamed about. We will be writing and reading about science, our community, and all the things of interest to your child. I look forward to the opportunity to work with your child and help open the doors to lifelong learning.

One of the areas we will be involved in and you will see the most growth in is writing. First grade children come to me with lots of stories to tell. My goal is to encourage children to write their stories. I want the children to come to view themselves as writers and conveyers of information. As your child begins to write, his/her first attempts may look somewhat unconventional. You will see single letters and beginning and ending consonants to signify whole words. Do not be alarmed. This is a natural developmental process of spelling and writing. We will work on sound–symbol relationships as the children begin to use more and more words in their writing.

My instruction will occur on a daily basis with individual children as well as small groups and large group. Phonics will be taught in the context of the children's writing as they "invent" the spellings for the sounds they hear. We will be engaged in lots of reading—I will read aloud many times during the day; children will read silently, in pairs, and in small groups. It is through reading and writing with purpose that your child will come to understand the meaning of print and be able to use print to communicate messages to audiences.

I invite you to come be a part of our classroom. Be involved with your child as she/he is learning about print in both reading and writing.

I encourage you to read to your child each night and allow your child to read to you. Write with your child as often as possible. Allow your child to share his/her stories with you and give encouragement as he/she struggles to develop a sense of communication in writing.

I believe you will be amazed at the progress your child will make as the school year progresses. Single letters and consonants only will be replaced by full words as children come to understand the relationship between sounds and symbols. Again, I look forward to the school year with your child.

Sincerely,


Barbara Long

# APPENDIX 2

# Monthly Writing Checklist

Name _____

| | Comments | Date |
|---|---|---|
| Uses scribble writing | | |
| Attempts invented spelling | | |
| Illustrations match text | | |
| Writes from left to right | | |
| Uses beginning sounds | | |
| Uses ending sounds | | |
| Uses medial consonants | | |
| Uses vowel sounds | | |
| Knows letter names | | |

| | Comments | Date |
|---|---|---|
| Knows letter sounds | | |
| Uses sight words | | |
| Sequences ideas | | |
| Responds to assigned topics | | |
| Uses capital letters | | |
| Uses periods | | |
| Uses question marks | | |
| Recognizes mistakes | | |
| Uses spaces between words | | |
| Uses writing spontaneously | | |
| Uses written resources | | |
| Number of sentences in writing | | |
| Varies topics | | |

# APPENDIX 3

# Sample Lesson Plan Using Children's Literature (Rehearsal)

**Topic of Lesson**  Finding a topic

**Lesson Objective**  Students will relate a story found in a piece of literature to their own lives.

**Procedures**
1. Read *Wilford Gordon McDonald Partridge* by Mem Fox.

2. Stop periodically and ask children about their memories of something soft, something of value, something that makes them cry, something that makes them laugh, and something fragile.

3. After book has been read, ask children to think about the things the story reminded them of in their own lives. Allow children to tell of their memories.

4. On chart paper, write the memories children tell.

5. Tell children to look over the list written on the chart paper and tell a neighbor what they might write about today.

6. Children will get out their writing notebooks and begin writing.

# Sample Craft/Skill Lesson Plan Using Children's Literature

**Topic of Lesson**    Use of simile and metaphor

**Lesson Objective**

1. Students will identify a simile and a metaphor.
2. Students will use similes and metaphors in their writing in order to make their writing come alive.

**Procedures**

1. Read *Owl Moon* by Jane Yolen. Instruct students to listen to the beautiful language used.
2. Ask students what they heard as they listened. What were they able to see? How did Yolen make us "see" and "hear" the words?
3. Explain to students the meaning of the term *simile*. Tell students why authors use similes in writing.
4. Explain to students the meaning of the term *metaphor*. Tell students why authors use metaphors in writing.
5. Find examples of both simile and metaphor in *Owl Moon* and discuss how they help the reader visualize the story.
6. Make a chart with two columns—one for similes and one for metaphors. Invite students, as they read other books, to add to the chart similes and metaphors that they find.
7. Have students look at their own writing and find places where similes or metaphors might be used effectively.
8. Share with the whole class.

**Assessment**    Observe individual students' use of similes and metaphors in their writing. Hold individual conferences with students and ask questions about their use of similes and metaphors.

*Copyright © 2000 by Allyn and Bacon.*

# APPENDIX 5

# Skills I Can Use as a Writer

Name _____

| Date | Skills I Can Use |
|------|------------------|
|      |                  |
|      |                  |
|      |                  |
|      |                  |
|      |                  |
|      |                  |
|      |                  |
|      |                  |

# APPENDIX 6

# Writing Record

Name _____

| Date | What I worked on today | What I want to work on tomorrow |
|------|------------------------|--------------------------------|
|      |                        |                                |
|      |                        |                                |
|      |                        |                                |
|      |                        |                                |
|      |                        |                                |
|      |                        |                                |
|      |                        |                                |
|      |                        |                                |
|      |                        |                                |

# APPENDIX 7

# My Writing Record

Name _____

| Date | I can do these things well | I'm working on these things | I plan to learn these things |
|------|----------------------------|-----------------------------|------------------------------|
|      |                            |                             |                              |
|      |                            |                             |                              |
|      |                            |                             |                              |
|      |                            |                             |                              |
|      |                            |                             |                              |
|      |                            |                             |                              |
|      |                            |                             |                              |
|      |                            |                             |                              |
|      |                            |                             |                              |

# APPENDIX 8

# Anecdotal Records

Writer's name _____

Observation date _____

Observation time _____

Cognitive (thinking, reasoning, problem solving)

Knowledge of writing

Communication (use of written language)

Affective (expression of feelings, ability to handle frustrations and conflict)

Social interaction (seeking help from peers, conference skills, responses)

Creativity (use of imagination, description, and detail)

# APPENDIX 9

# Peer Conference Summary

Name _____ Date _____

Project title _____

Conference partners _____

1. What is my story/project about? _____

   _____

2. What do you like best about it? _____

   _____

3. Did I say anything confusing? What? _____

   _____

4. Do I need to add more details? Where? _____

   ☐ beginning      ☐ characters      ☐ plot

   ☐ setting        ☐ project design  ☐ ending

   Summary _____

   _____

   _____

# APPENDIX 10

# Community-Building Ideas

1. **"ALL ABOUT ME"** bulletin board—Each student brings in pictures and/or artifacts about his or her life; the student introduces him- or herself and places the items on the bulletin board. The board becomes a collage of the students.

2. **MUSEUM**—A place is set aside in the room as a museum of students' lives; one or two students per week bring in artifacts that say, "This is who I am"; the artifacts are placed in the museum and the students becomes the curators for the week; other students visit the museum and ask questions of the curators.

3. **AUTOBIOGRAPHICAL POEMS**—Students create poems that tell about their lives; poems are then shared and displayed in the room. The format of the poem is as follows:

> First name
> Daughter/son of . . .
> Sister/brother of . . .
> Loves (3 things) . . .
> Hates (3 things) . . .
> Feels (3 things) . . .
> Fears (3 things) . . .
> Would like to see . . .
> Street address
> Town
> Last name

4. **PERSONAL CINQUAIN**—Students create cinquains about who they are; poems are shared and displayed in the room. The format of the poem is as follows:

> First name
> 2 words that describe you
> 3 words ending in -ing that describe you
> A phrase that describes you
> A synonym for you

5. **MY LIFE IN A SUITCASE**—Teacher brings in a suitcase full of things that tell about who she/he is; teacher talks about the things and how they represent her/him; each student takes the suitcase home and brings it back with items representing him/herself.

6. **NAME GAME**—Students stand in a circle around the room; the first person begins by telling her/his name; each successive person must introduce him/herself and tell the preceding persons' names.

7. **INTERVIEWS**—Students are paired to interview another person; the interviewer asks the interviewee a series of questions in order to find out more about the person; interviews are written and a class newspaper is produced containing the interviews.

8. **FIND THE PERSON**—each student is given a list of questions and/or statements; the object is to meet every person in the room by finding out the answers to the questions. Examples of questions might be:

> Favorite song
> Favorite food
> Favorite movie
> Place you go to be alone
> Favorite vacation spot
> Most embarrassing moment
> Most admired person
> Favorite subject in school
> Favorite season
> Favorite author

# APPENDIX 11

# Check Your Story

☐ Each sentence begins with a capital.

☐ "I" is always capitalized.

☐ Each sentence ends with correct punctuation ("." "?" "!").

☐ The names of people and important places are capitalized.

☐ Quotation marks (". . .") are used to show when someone is talking.

☐ Each new paragraph is indented.

☐ I have checked to see that my story makes sense.

☐ My handwriting is clear and legible.

# APPENDIX 12

# Editor's Review

Type of writing _____

Title of literary piece _____

Author _____

Yes No

☐ ☐   1.  Did the title "catch your eye"? _____

_____

☐ ☐   2.  Did the title pertain to the subject? _____

_____

☐ ☐   3.  Were capital letters used correctly? _____

_____

☐ ☐   4.  Was there good paragraph structure? _____

_____

Yes  No

☐    ☐    5.   Were all the words spelled/used (to, too, two) correctly? _____

_____

☐    ☐    6.   Was the punctuation (including dialogue) used correctly? _____

_____

☐    ☐    7.   Were there errors in grammar? If so, please list examples.
              Remember to check subject/verb agreement. _____

_____

☐    ☐    8.   If it applies to the writing, was the scene set correctly
              (who, where, and when)? _____

_____

☐    ☐    9.   Did the beginning capture your attention and make you
              want to continue reading? _____

_____

☐    ☐    10.  Did you understand what the author was trying to express in his/her writing?
              Why or why not? _____

_____

☐    ☐    11.  Did the author's work have a good ending/conclusion?
              What did you like or not like about the work? _____

_____

Yes   No

☐    ☐    12.   What sentence/line was the most effective sentence/line written by

the author in this work? _____

Editor's signature (May be parent, teacher, peer, volunteer, or older relative) _____

_____

Date edited _____

Additional comments? _____

_____

_____

_____

_____

_____

# APPENDIX 13

# Skills Checklist

*Directions:* Using your writing piece for this six weeks, find an example of the listed skill and copy it:

1. Declarative sentence: _____

2. Interrogative sentence: _____

3. Imperative sentence: _____

4. A sentence with a compound subject: _____

_____

5. A sentence with a compound predicate: _____

_____

6. A compound sentence: _____

_____

7. A sentence with a concrete noun: _____

8. A sentence with a proper noun: _____

9. A sentence using a plural noun that does not end in *s*: _____

_____

10. A sentence using a collective noun: _____

_____

11. A sentence with an appositive: _____

_____

12. In the space below, list at least ten spelling words found in the five spelling units we have
covered. These words must be in your writing sample. _____

_____

_____

_____

_____

_____

_____

_____

_____

_____

_____

_____

# APPENDIX 14

# Writing Rubric

Name _____

Date _____

Title of piece _____

| Category | Consistent | Inconsistent | Not Applicable |
|---|---|---|---|
| Writes a draft that is understandable | | | |
| Accepts suggestions made by peers and teacher | | | |
| Attempts to use descriptive language | | | |
| Takes responsibility for revision | | | |
| Edits final draft | | | |
| Accepts responsibility for deadlines | | | |
| Asks for conferences | | | |
| Drafts and revisions are easily located in the writing folder | | | |

| Category | Consistent | Inconsistent | Not Applicable |
|---|---|---|---|
| Final piece is written neatly and legibly | | | |
| Takes pride in writing | | | |

Scoring System:    A  =  consistent in all areas (9 out of 10)
                    B  =  consistent in most areas (8 out of 10)
                    C  =  consistent in many areas (7 out of 10)
                    D  =  consistent in some areas (6 out of 10)
                    F  =  inconsistent in many areas (3 or less out of 10)

Final Grade _____

# Children's Literature Used at Various Stages of the Writing Process

## Rehearsal

Brown, M. (1996). *Arthur Writes a Story*. New York: Scholastic.

Carlstrom, N. W. (1990). *Grandpappy*. New York: Little, Brown.

Fleming, V. (1993). *Be Good to Eddie Lee*. New York: Philomel Books.

Fox, M. (1984). *Wilford Gordon McDonald Partridge*. New York: Trumpet Club.

Hamilton, V. (1993). *Plain City*. New York: Scholastic.

Hazbry, N. & Condy, R. (1983). *How to Get Rid of Bad Dreams*. New York: Scholastic.

Henkes, K. (1991). *Chrysanthemum*. New York: Trumpet Club.

Hurd, T. (1985). *Mama Don't Allow*. New York: HarperCollins Children's Books.

Pollaco, P. (1988). *The Keeping Quilt*. New York: Trumpet Club.

Pollaco, P. (1992). *Chicken Sunday*. New York: Philomel Books.

Pollaco, P. (1994). *My Rotten Red-Headed Older Brother*. New York: Trumpet Club.

Pollaco, P. (1995). *My Ol' Man*. New York: Scholastic.

Mochizuki, K. (1993). *Baseball Saved Us*. New York: Lee & Low Books.

Munsch, R. (1980). *The Paper Bag Princess*. Toronto, Ont.: Annick Press.

Munsch, R. (1986). *Love You Forever*. Ont.: Firefly Books.

Munsch, R. (1987). *Moira's Birthday*. Toronto, Ont.: Annick Press.

Rylant, C. (1982). *When I Was Young in the Mountains*. New York: Puffin Unicorn.

Rylant, C. (1985). *The Relatives Came*. New York: Scholastic.

Stewart, S. (1991). *The Money Tree*. New York: Farrar, Straus & Giroux.

Wilhelm, H. (1985). *I Will Always Love You*. New York: Scholastic.

Williams, K. H. (1990). *Galimoto*. New York: Trumpet Club.

# Literary Craft

### Figurative Language

Base, G. (1986). *Animalia*. New York: Harry N. Abrams.
Fox, M. (1989). *Night Noises*. New York: Trumpet Club.
Merriam, E. (1991). *The Wise Woman and Her Secret*. New York: Simon & Schuster.
Yolen, J. (1987). *Owl Moon*. New York: Scholastic.

### Beginnings

Blaine, M. (1975). *The Terrible Thing that Happened at Our House*. Parent's Magazine.
Cherry, L. (1990). *The Great Kapok Tree*. New York: Trumpet Club.
Lionni, L. (1969). *Alexander and the Wind-up Mouse*. New York: Knopf.
Mazer, A. (1991). *The Salamander Room*. New York: Random House.
Van Allsburg, C. (1984). *The Mysteries of Harris Burdick*. Boston: Houghton Mifflin.
Van Allsburg, C. (1990). *Just a Dream*. New York: Scholastic.

### Theme/Plot

Blake, R. J. (1981). *Dog*. New York: Philomel Books.
Bunting, E. (1994). *Smokey Night*. New York: Harcourt Brace.
Fox, M. (1984). *Feathers and Fools*. New York: Harcourt Brace.
Seuss, D. (1990). *Oh, the Places You'll Go!*. New York: Random House.
Shannon, D. (1994). *How Georgie Radbourn Saved Baseball*. New York: Blue Sky Press.
Van Allsburg, C. (1981). *Jumanji*. Boston: Houghton Mifflin.

### Point of View

Ets, M. H. (1965). *Just Me*. New York: Viking Press.
Goble, P. (1978). *The Girl Who Loved Horses*. New York: Bradbury Press.
Pittman, H. C. (1988). *Once When I Was Scared*. New York: Dutton.
Scueszka, J. (1996). *The True Story of the 3 Little Pigs*. New York: Puffin Books.
Van Allsburg, C. (1988). *Two Bad Ants*. Boston: Houghton Mifflin.
Viorst, J. (1987). *Alexander and the Terrible, Horrible, No Good, Very Bad Day*. New York: Scholastic.

### Character Development

Freedman, F. B. (1971). *Two Tickets to Freedom*. New York: Scholastic.
Hahn, M. D. (1991). *Stepping on Crack*. New York: Clarion Books.

### Conclusions

MacLachlan, P. (1991). *Journey*. New York: Dell.
Wier, E. (1963). *The Loner*. New York: Scholastic.
Yolen, J. (1987). *Owl Moon*. New York: Scholastic.

### Poetry and Other Genres

Climo, S. (1993). *Korean Cinderella*. New York: HarperCollins.
Mahy, M. (1990). *Seven Chinese Brothers*. New York: Scholastic.
Myers, W. D. (1997). *Harlem*. New York: Scholastic.
Wood, A. (1995). *The Rainbow Bridge*. San Diego, CA: Harcourt Brace.
Yolen, J. (1987). *Owl Moon*. New York: Philomel Books.
Young, E. (1989). *Lon Po Po*. New York: Scholastic.

## Skills and Conventions

### Punctuation

Dakos, K. (1995). *Mrs. Cole on an Onion Roll and Other School Poems*.
    New York: Trumpet Club.
Gwynne, F. (1988). *A Little Pigeon Toad*. New York: Trumpet Club.
Meddaugh, S. (1994). *Martha Calling*. New York: Houghton Mifflin.
Thomas, P. (1971). *"Stand Back," Said the Elephant, "I'm Going to
    Sneeze!"*. New York: Lothrop, Lee & Shepard.

### Punctuation

Munsch, R. (1991). *Show and Tell*. Toronto, Ont.: Annick Press.

### Dialogue

Bunting, E. (1990). *The Wall*. New York: Clarion Books.
McKissack, P. (1989). *Nettie Jo's Friend*. New York: Knopf.

Waber, B. (1972). *Ira Sleeps Over*. New York: Scholastic.
Waber, B. (1988). *Ira Says Goodbye*. New York: Scholastic.

### Parts of Speech

Bunting, E. (1996). *The Secret Place*. New York: Clarion Books
Caudill, R. (1964). *A Pocketful of Cricket*. Holt, Rinehart & Winston.
Heller, R. (1987). *A Cache of Jewels*. New York: Scholastic.
Heller, R. (1988). *Kites Sail High*. New York: Grosset & Dunlap.
Heller, R. (1989). *Many Luscious Lollipops*. New York: Grossett & Dunlap.
Heller, R. (1989). *Up, Up, and Away*. New York: Grossett & Dunlap.
Heller, R. (1990). *Merry-Go-Round*. New York: Grosset & Dunlap.

# Index